FOR ORGANS, PIANOS & ELECTRONIC KEYBOARDS

E-Z PLAY® TODAY

65

HYMNS
WITH 3 CHORDS

T0057171

ISBN 978-1-4234-0275-6

HAL•LEONARD®
CORPORATION
7777 W. BLUEMOUND RD. P.O.BOX 13819 MILWAUKEE, WI 53213

In Australia Contact:
Hal Leonard Australia Pty. Ltd.
4 Lentara Court
Cheltenham, Victoria, 3192 Australia
Email: ausadmin@halleonard.com

Visit Hal Leonard Online at
www.halleonard.com

CONTENTS

4   Amazing Grace
6   At the Cross
8   Battle Hymn of the Republic
10 Beautiful Savior
11 Blest Be the Tie That Binds
12 Come, Christians, Join to Sing
14 Count Your Blessings
16 Faith of Our Fathers
18 For the Beauty of the Earth
20 Guide Me, O Thou Great Jehovah
22 Have Thine Own Way, Lord
24 He Leadeth Me
13 How Firm a Foundation
26 I Am Thine, O Lord
28 I Sing the Mighty Power of God
30 I Surrender All
32 Jesus, Keep Me Near the Cross
34 Jesus Shall Reign
36 Joyful, Joyful, We Adore Thee
38 Just As I Am
40 Leaning on the Everlasting Arms
42 My Jesus, I Love Thee
44 Near to the Heart of God
46 Nearer, My God, to Thee
35 O Worship the King
48 Only Trust Him
49 Praise to the Lord, the Almighty
50 Savior, Like a Shepherd Lead Us
51 Stand Up, Stand Up for Jesus
52 Standing on the Promises
54 Sweet Hour of Prayer
56 This Is My Father's World
58 'Tis So Sweet to Trust in Jesus
59 What a Friend We Have in Jesus
62 When I Survey the Wondrous Cross
60 Wonderful Words of Life

63 **REGISTRATION GUIDE**

Amazing Grace

Registration 1
Rhythm: Waltz

Words by John Newton
Traditional American Melody

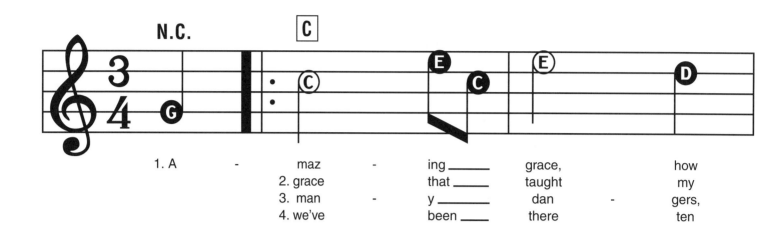

1. A	-	maz	-	ing ____	grace,		how
2. grace		that ____		taught			my
3. man	-	y ____		dan	-		gers,
4. we've		been ____		there			ten

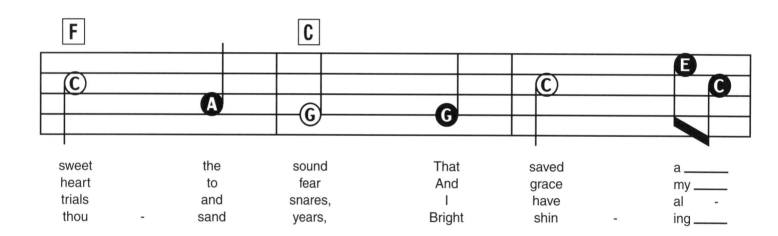

sweet	the	sound	That	saved	a ____	
heart	to	fear	And	grace	my ____	
trials	and	snares,	I	have	al	-
thou	- sand	years,	Bright	shin	- ing ____	

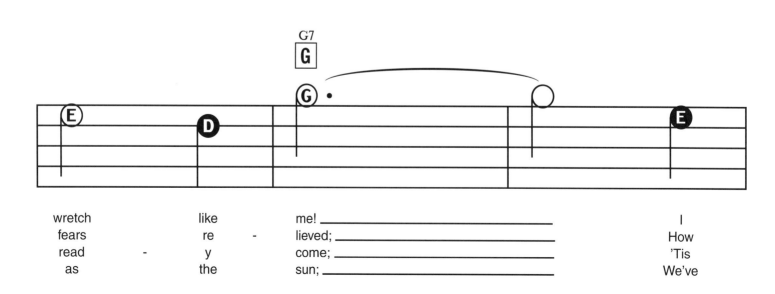

wretch	like	me! ____		I
fears	re -	lieved; ____		How
read	- y	come; ____		'Tis
as	the	sun; ____		We've

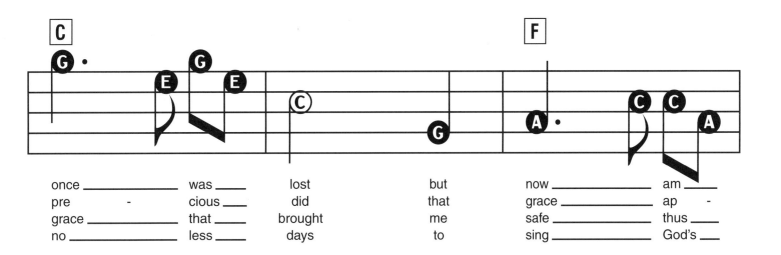

once	was	lost	but	now	am
pre -	cious	did	that	grace	ap -
grace	that	brought	me	safe	thus
no	less	days	to	sing	God's

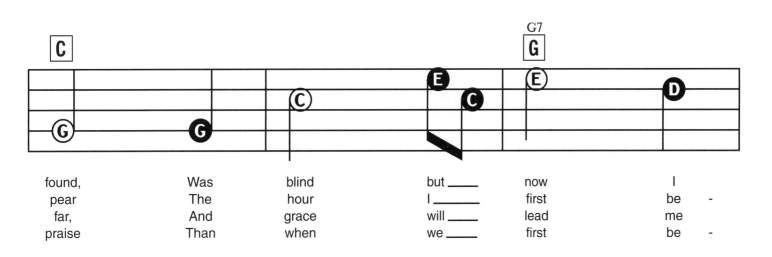

found,	Was	blind	but	now	I
pear	The	hour	I	first	be -
far,	And	grace	will	lead	me
praise	Than	when	we	first	be -

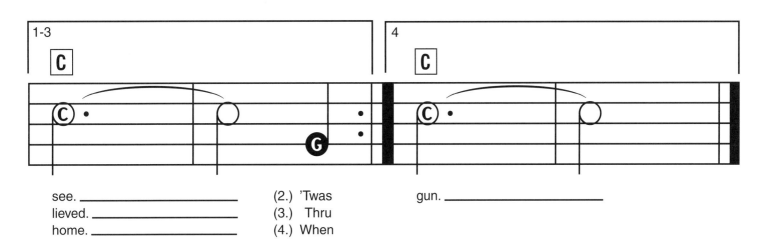

1-3		4	
see.	(2.) 'Twas	gun.	
lieved.	(3.) Thru		
home.	(4.) When		

At the Cross

Registration 2
Rhythm: Ballad or Fox Trot

Words by Isaac Watts and Ralph E. Hudson
Music by Ralph E. Hudson

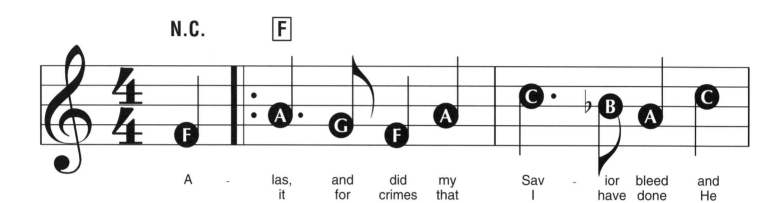

A - las, and did my Sav - ior bleed and
it for did crimes my that I have done He

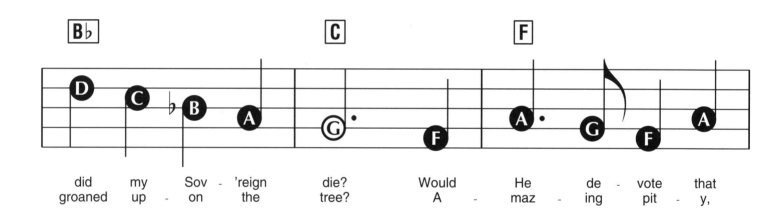

did my Sov - 'reign die? Would He de - vote that
groaned up - on the tree? A - maz - ing pit - y,

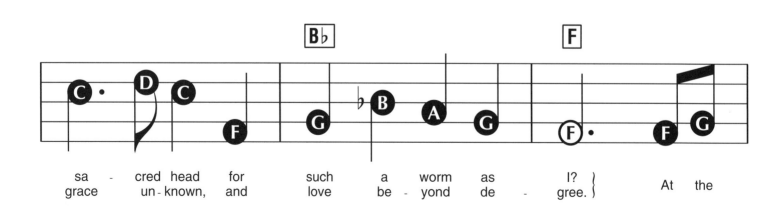

sa - cred head for such a worm as I? At the
grace un - known, and love be - yond de - gree.

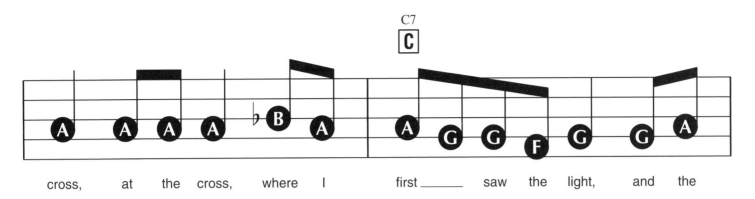

cross, at the cross, where I first _____ saw the light, and the

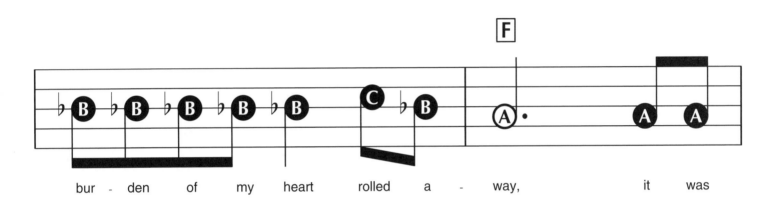

bur - den of my heart rolled a - way, it was

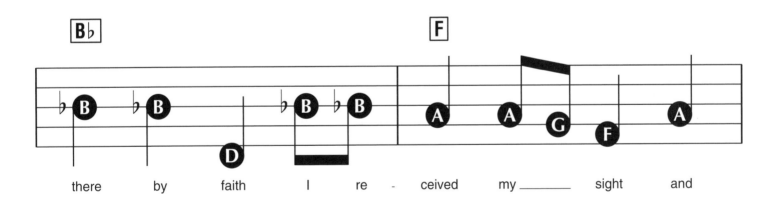

there by faith I re - ceived my _____ sight and

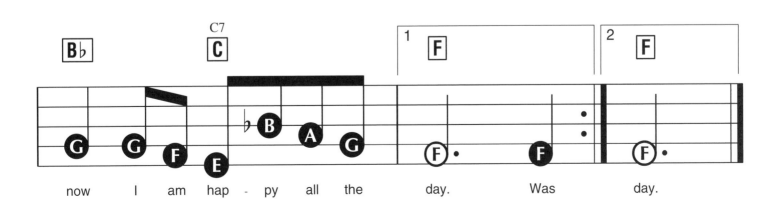

now I am hap - py all the day. Was day.

Battle Hymn of the Republic

Registration 7
Rhythm: March

Words by Julia Ward Howe
Music by William Steffe

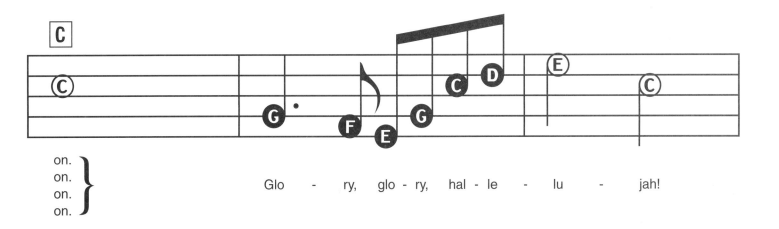

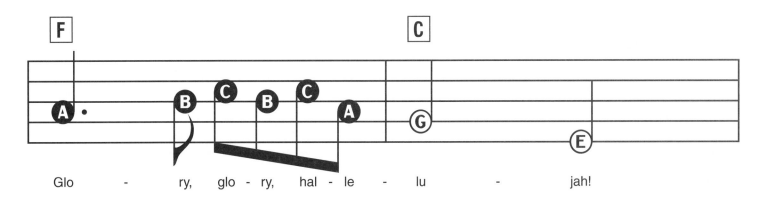

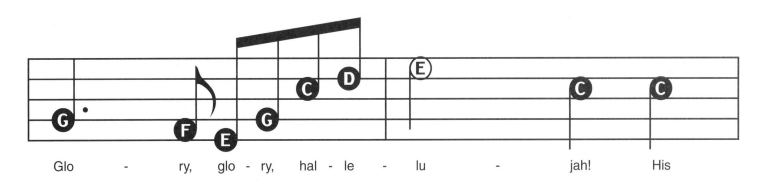

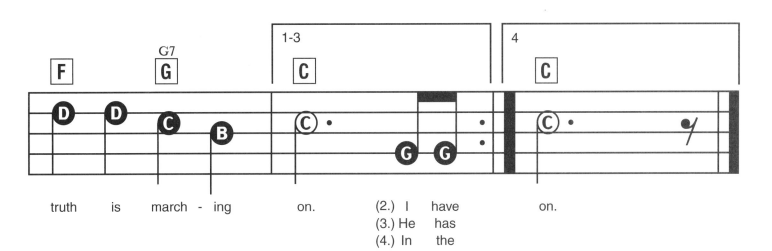

Beautiful Savior

Registration 3
Rhythm: None

Words from *Munsterisch Gesangbuch*
Translated by Joseph A. Seiss
Music adapted from Silesian Folk Tune

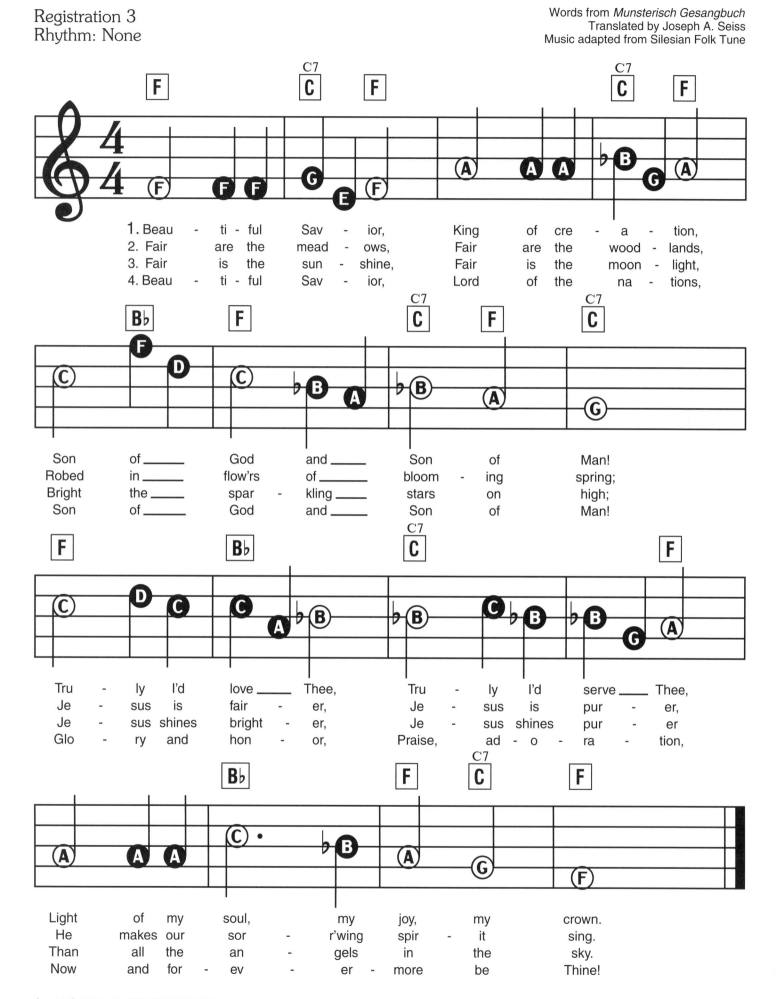

Blest Be the Tie That Binds

Registration 8
Rhythm: Waltz

Words by John Fawcett
Music by Johann G. Nägeli
Arranged by Lowell Mason

1. Blest be the tie that binds Our
2. Be - fore our Fa - ther's throne We
3. We share each oth - er's woes, Our
4. When we a - sun - der part, It

hearts in Chris - tian love; The
pour our ar - dent prayers; Our
mu - tual bur - dens bear; And
gives us in - ward pain; But

fel - low - ship of kin - dred minds Is
fears, our hopes, our aims are one, Our
of - ten for each oth - er flows The
we shall still be joined in heart, And

like to that a - bove.
com - forts and our cares.
sym - pa - thiz - ing tear.
hope to meet a - gain.

Come, Christians, Join to Sing

Registration 3
Rhythm: Fox Trot

Words by Christian Henry Bateman
Traditional Spanish Melody

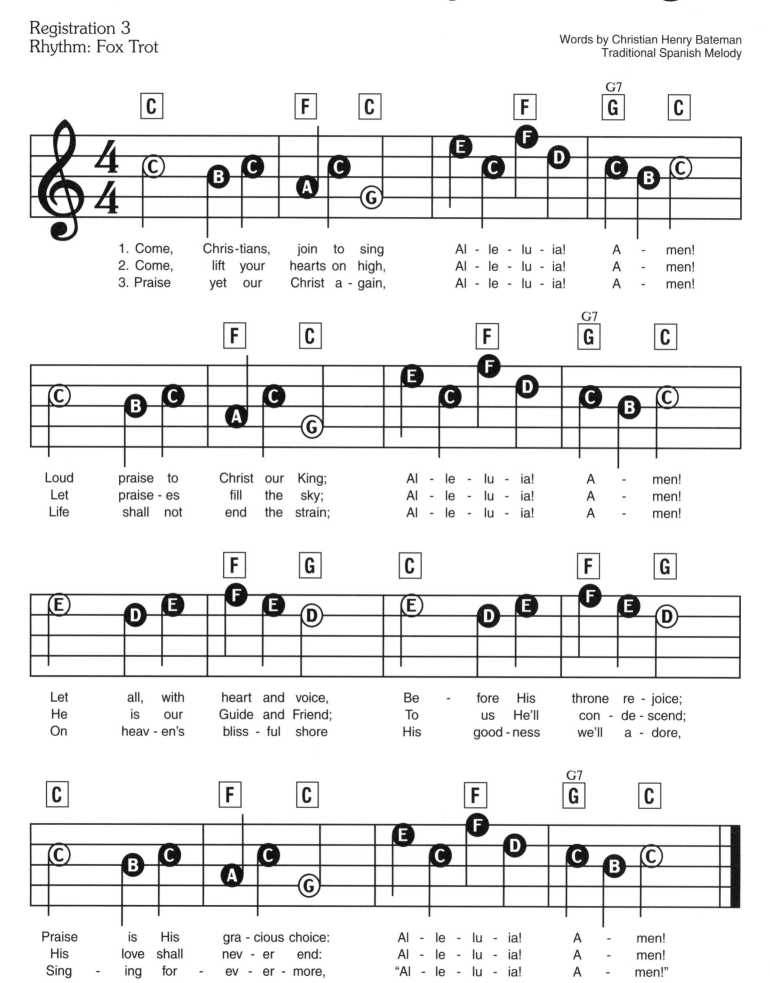

1. Come, Chris-tians, join to sing Al - le - lu - ia! A - men!
2. Come, lift your hearts on high, Al - le - lu - ia! A - men!
3. Praise yet our Christ a - gain, Al - le - lu - ia! A - men!

Loud praise to Christ our King; Al - le - lu - ia! A - men!
Let praise - es fill the sky; Al - le - lu - ia! A - men!
Life shall not end the strain; Al - le - lu - ia! A - men!

Let all, with heart and voice, Be - fore His throne re - joice;
He is our Guide and Friend; To us He'll con - de - scend;
On heav - en's bliss - ful shore His good - ness we'll a - dore,

Praise is His gra - cious choice: Al - le - lu - ia! A - men!
His love shall nev - er end: Al - le - lu - ia! A - men!
Sing - ing for - ev - er - more, "Al - le - lu - ia! A - men!"

How Firm a Foundation

Registration 3
Rhythm: Fox Trot

Words by John Rippon's *A Selection of Hymns*
Early American Melody

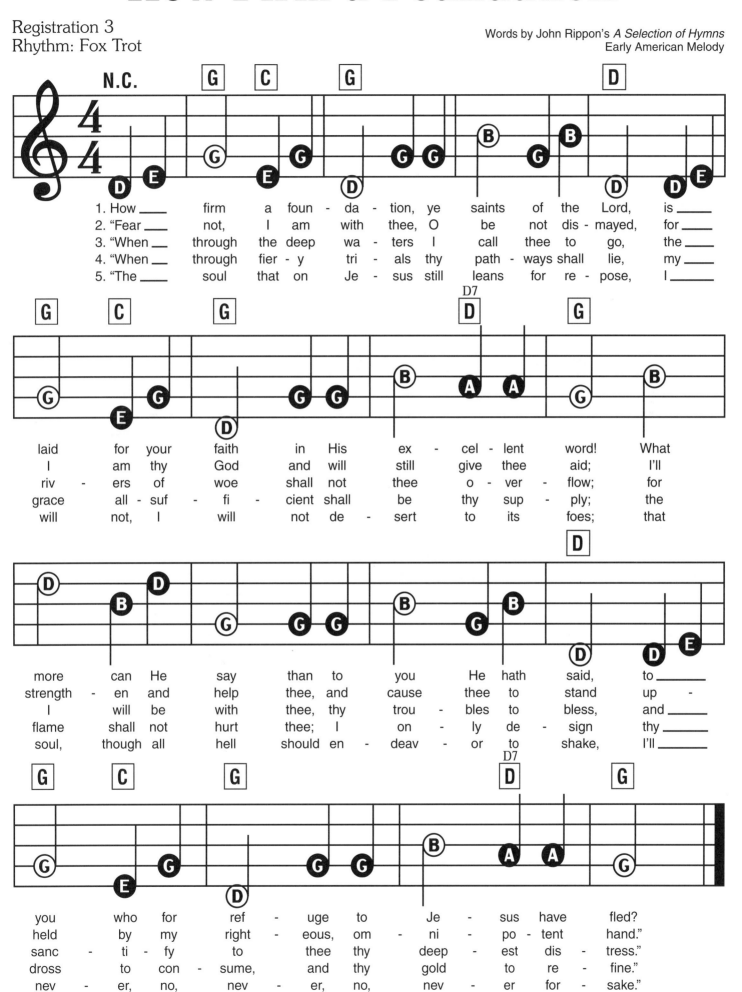

1. How firm a foun - da - tion, ye saints of the Lord, is laid for your faith in His ex - cel - lent word! What more can He say than to you He hath said, to you who for ref - uge to Je - sus have fled?
2. "Fear not, I am with thee, O be not dis - mayed, for I am thy God and will still give thee aid; I'll strength - en and help thee, and cause thee to stand up - held by my right - eous, om - ni - po - tent hand."
3. "When through the deep wa - ters I call thee to go, the riv - ers of woe shall not thee o - ver - flow; for I will be with thee, thy trou - bles to bless, and sanc - ti - fy to thee thy deep - est dis - tress."
4. "When through fier - y tri - als thy path - ways shall lie, my grace all - suf - fi - cient shall be thy sup - ply; the flame shall not hurt thee; I on - ly de - sign thy dross to con - sume, and thy gold to re - fine."
5. "The soul that on Je - sus still leans for re - pose, I will not, I will not de - sert to its foes; that soul, though all hell should en - deav - or to shake, I'll nev - er, no, nev - er, no, nev - er for - sake."

Count Your Blessings

Registration 2
Rhythm: Fox Trot

Words by Johnson Oatman, Jr.
Music by Edwin O. Excell

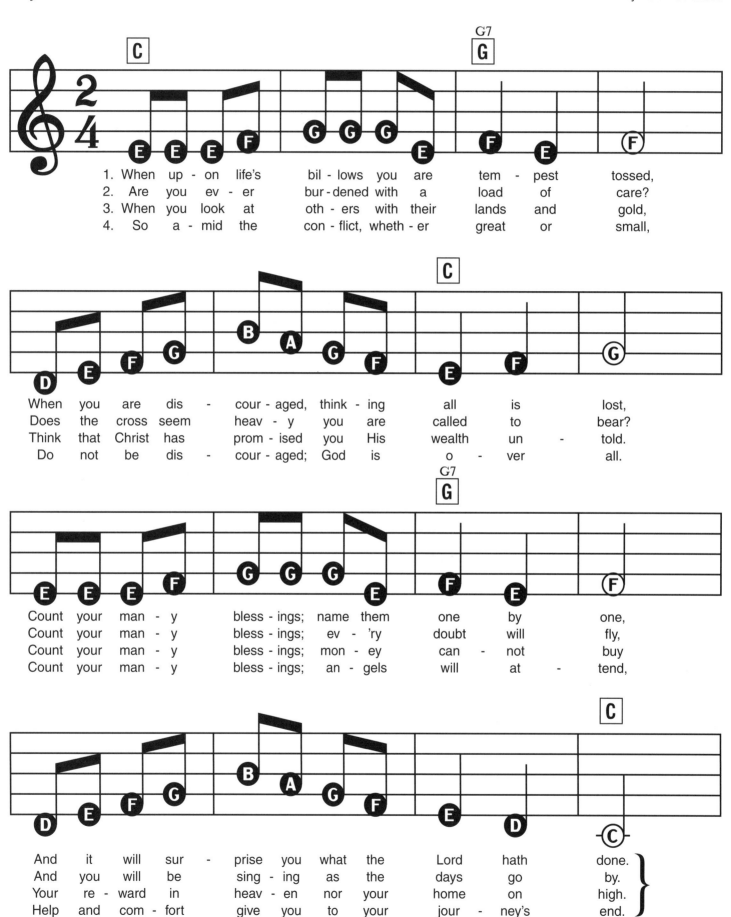

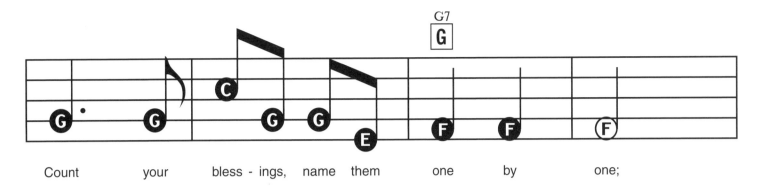

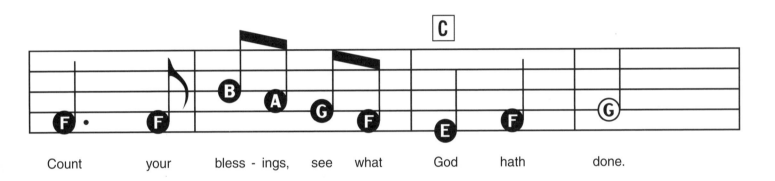

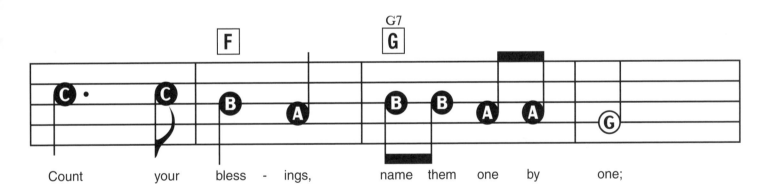

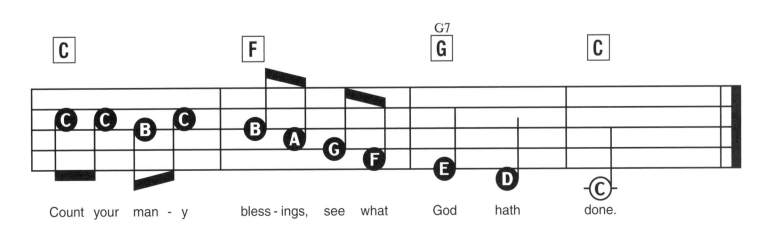

Faith of Our Fathers

Registration 2
Rhythm: Waltz

Words by Frederick William Faber
Music by Henri F. Hemy and James G. Walton

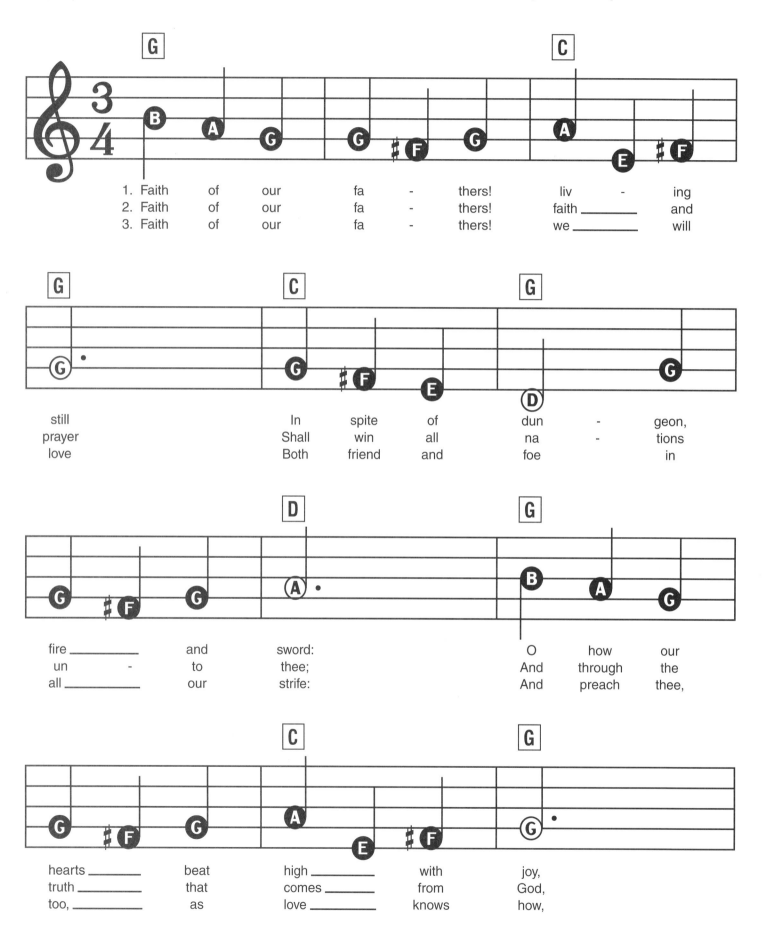

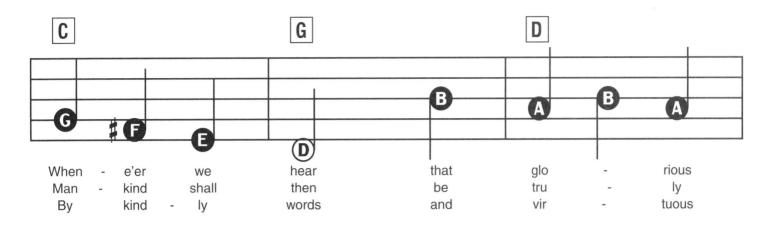

When - e'er we hear that glo - rious
Man - kind we shall then be tru - ly
By kind - ly words and vir - tuous

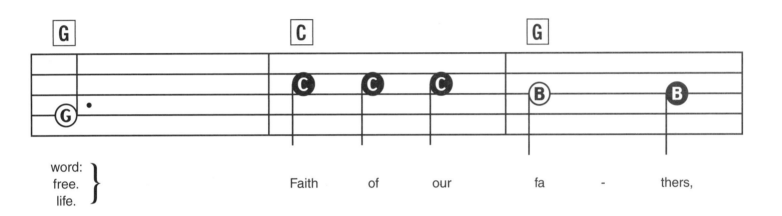

word:
free. }
life.

Faith of our fa - thers,

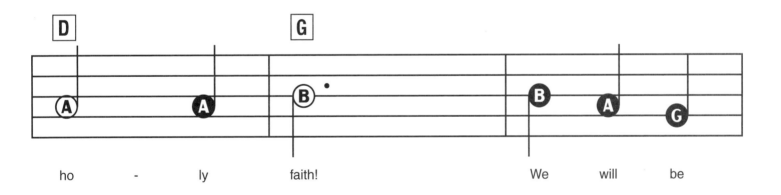

ho - ly faith! We will be

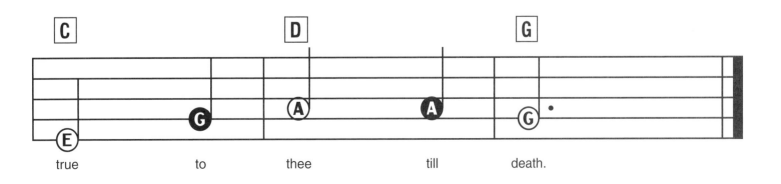

true to thee till death.

For the Beauty of the Earth

Registration 1
Rhythm: Ballad

Words by Folliot S. Pierpoint
Music by Conrad Kocher

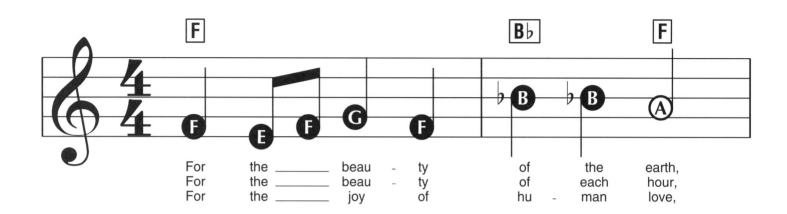

For	the	beau	ty	of	the	earth,
For	the	beau	ty	of	each	hour,
For	the	joy	of	hu - man		love,

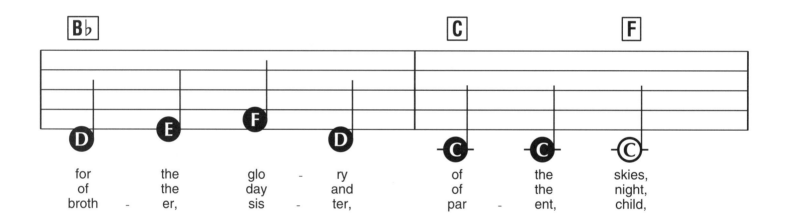

for	the	glo	ry	of	the	skies,
of	the	day	and	of	the	night,
broth - er,		sis	ter,	par -	ent,	child,

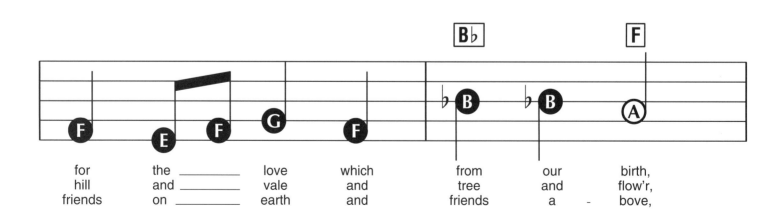

for	the	love	which	from	our	birth,
hill	and	vale	and	tree	and	flow'r,
friends	on	earth	and	friends	a -	bove,

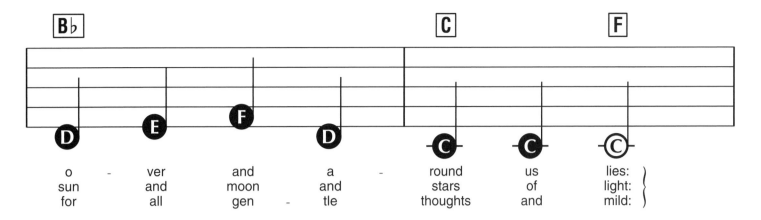

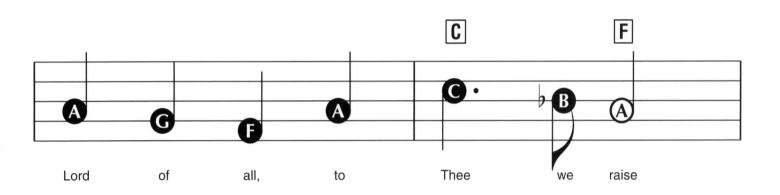

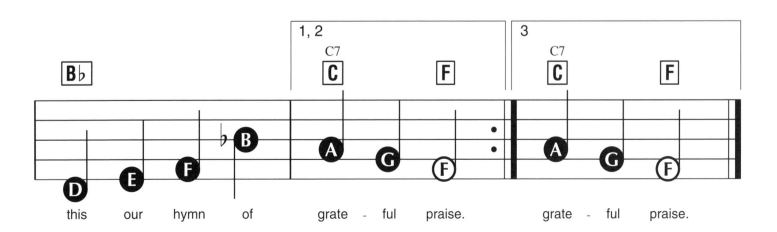

Guide Me, O Thou Great Jehovah

Registration 1
Rhythm: None

Words by William Williams
Music by John Hughes

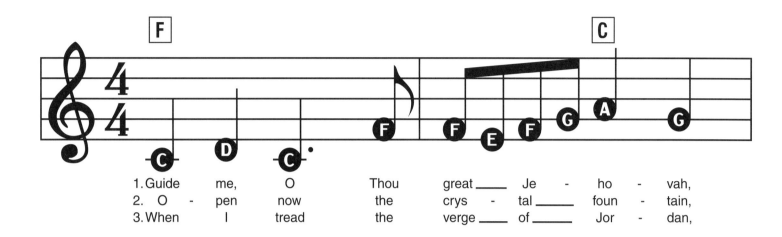

1. Guide	me,	O	Thou	great ____ Je -	ho -	vah,
2. O - pen	now	the	crys - tal ____	foun -	tain,
3. When I	tread	the	verge ____ of ____	Jor -	dan,

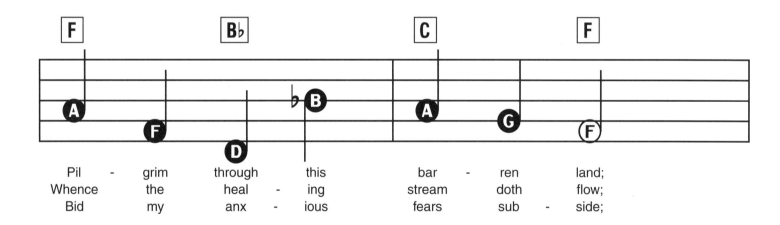

Pil -	grim	through	this	bar - ren	land;
Whence	the	heal -	ing	stream doth	flow;
Bid	my	anx -	ious	fears sub -	side;

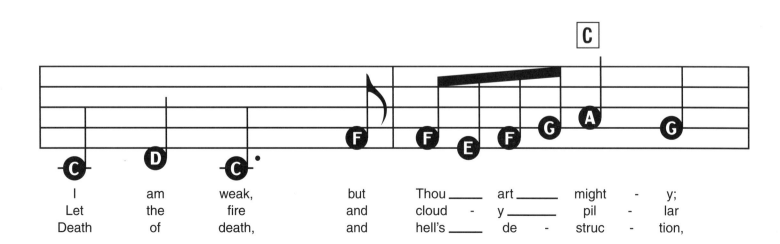

I	am	weak,	but	Thou ____ art ____ might -	y;
Let	the	fire	and	cloud - y ____ pil -	lar
Death	of	death,	and	hell's ____ de - struc -	tion,

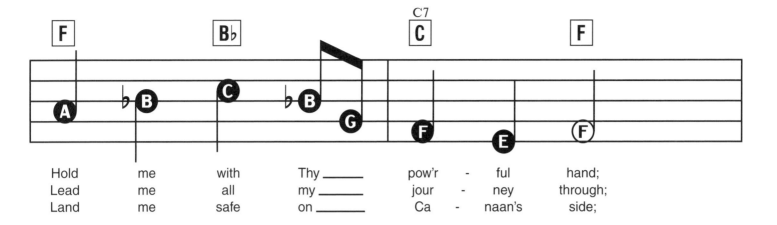

Hold me with Thy pow'r - ful hand;
Lead me all my jour - ney through;
Land me safe on Ca - naan's side;

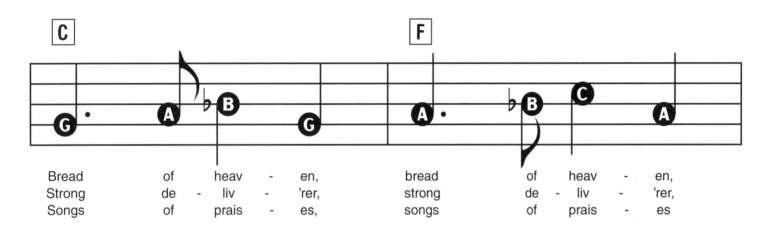

Bread of heav - en, bread of heav - en,
Strong de - liv - 'rer, strong de - liv - 'rer,
Songs of prais - es, songs of prais - es

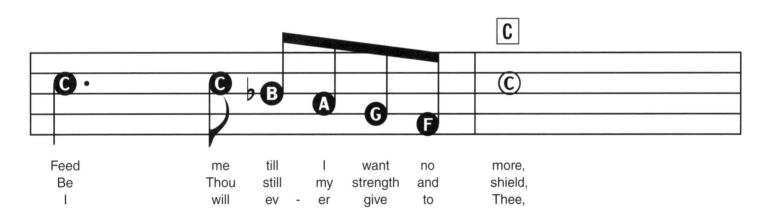

Feed me till I want no more,
Be Thou still my strength and shield,
I will ev - er give to Thee,

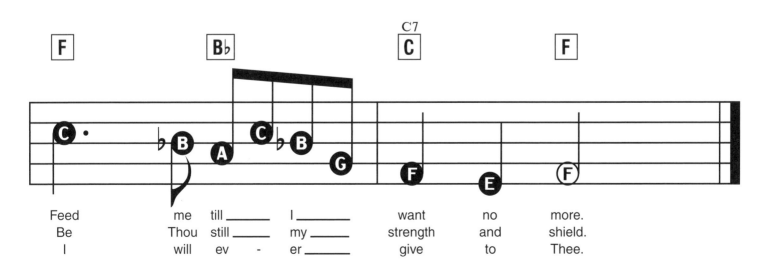

Feed me till I want no more.
Be Thou still my strength and shield.
I will ev - er give to Thee.

Have Thine Own Way, Lord

Registration 3
Rhythm: Waltz

Words by Adelaide A. Pollard
Music by George C. Stebbins

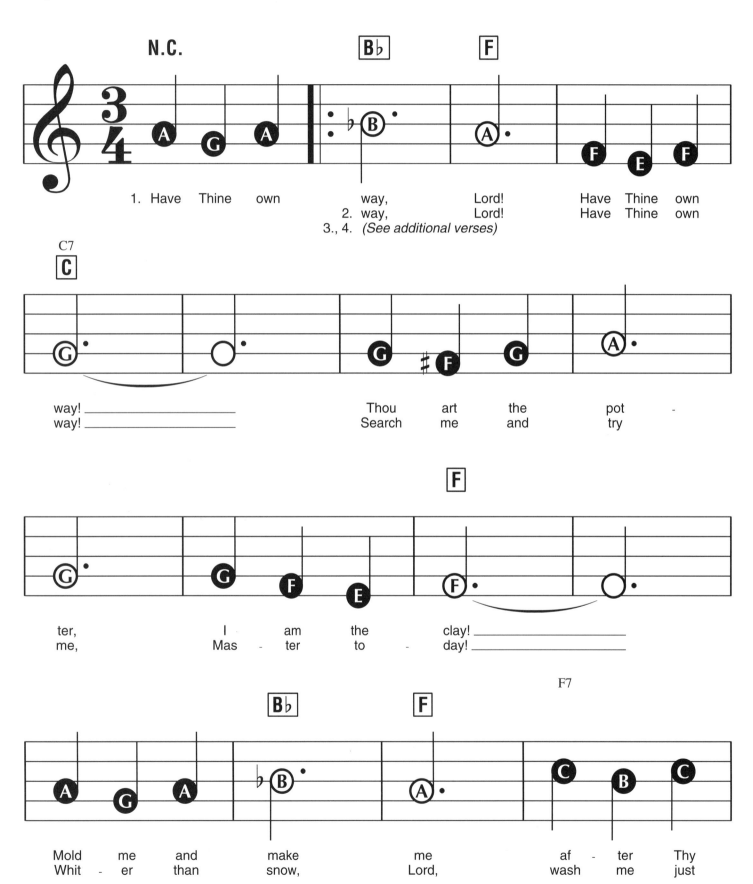

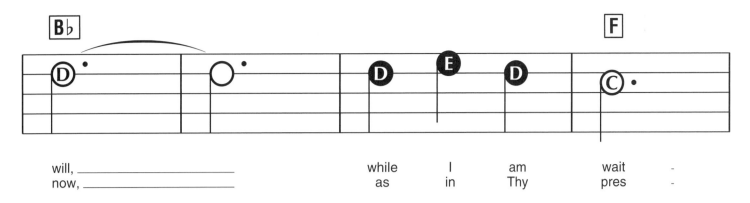

will, _____ while I am wait -
now, _____ as in Thy pres -

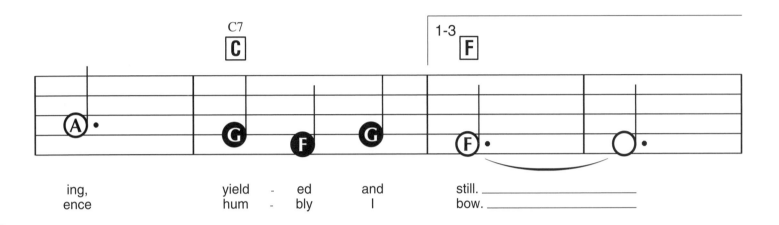

ing, yield - ed and still. _____
ence hum - bly I bow. _____

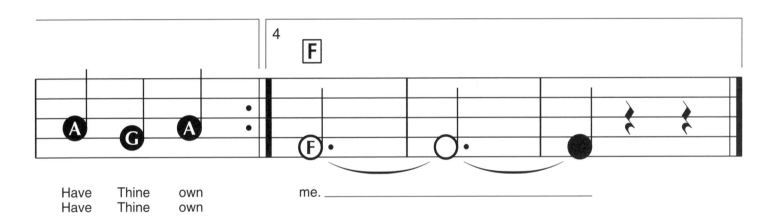

Have Thine own me. _____
Have Thine own

Additional Verses

3. Have Thine own way, Lord!
   Have Thine own way!
   Wounded and weary, Help me, I pray!
   Power, all power surely is Thine!
   Touch me and heal me, Savior divine.

4. Have Thine own way, Lord!
   Have Thine own way!
   Hold o'er me being Absolute sway!
   Fill with Thy Spirit till all shall see
   Christ only, always, Living in me.

He Leadeth Me

Registration 2
Rhythm: None

Words by Joseph H. Gilmore
Music by William B. Bradbury

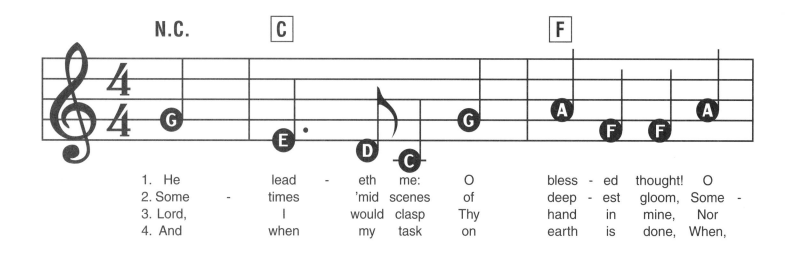

1. He   lead - eth me: O   bless - ed thought! O
2. Some - times   'mid scenes of   deep - est gloom, Some -
3. Lord,   I   would clasp Thy   hand in mine, Nor
4. And   when   my task on   earth is done, When,

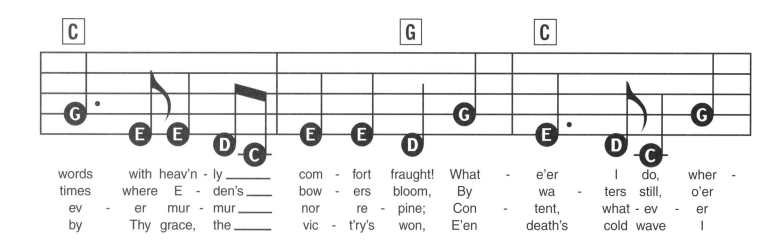

words   with heav'n - ly _____ com - fort fraught! What - e'er   I do, wher -
times   where E - den's ___ bow - ers bloom, By   wa - ters still, o'er
ev - er mur - mur _____ nor re - pine; Con - tent, what - ev - er
by   Thy grace, the _____ vic - t'ry's won, E'en   death's cold wave I

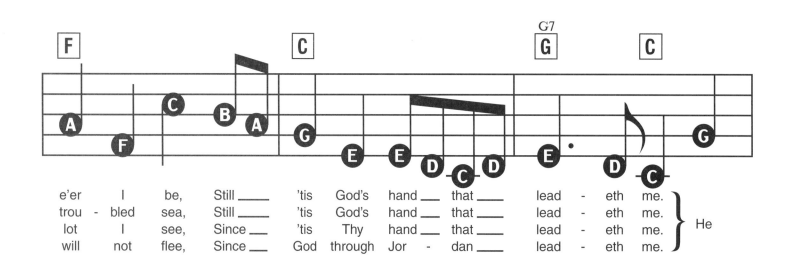

e'er   I be,   Still ___ 'tis God's hand ___ that ___ lead - eth me.
trou - bled sea,   Still ___ 'tis God's hand ___ that ___ lead - eth me.
lot   I see,   Since ___ 'tis Thy hand ___ that ___ lead - eth me.
will not flee,   Since ___ God through Jor - dan ___ lead - eth me.

He

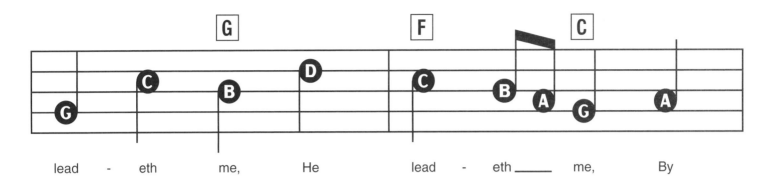

lead - eth me, He lead - eth _____ me, By

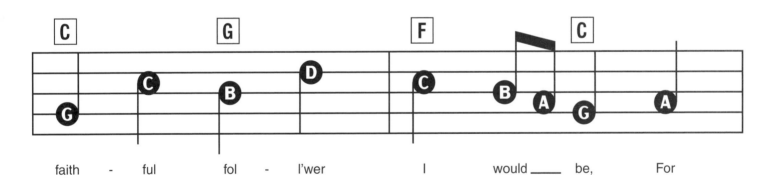

His own hand, _____ He _____ lead - eth me. His

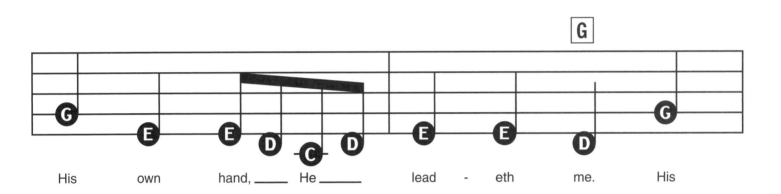

faith - ful fol - l'wer I would _____ be, For

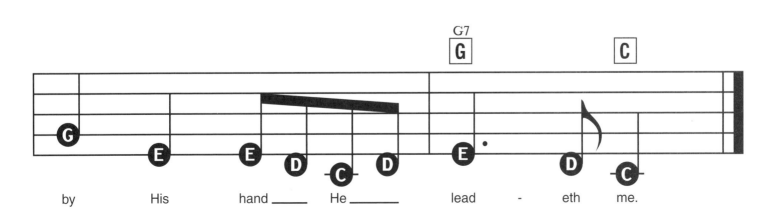

by His hand _____ He _____ lead - eth me.

I Am Thine, O Lord

Registration 2
Rhythm: Fox Trot

Words by Fanny J. Crosby
Music by William H. Doane

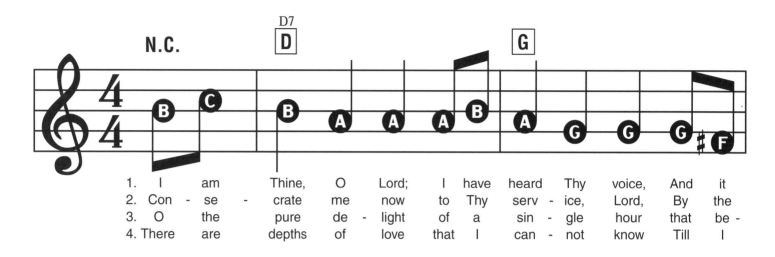

1. I am Thine, O Lord; I have heard Thy voice, And it
2. Con - se - crate me now to Thy serv - ice, Lord, By the
3. O the pure de - light of a sin - gle hour that be -
4. There are depths of love that I can - not know Till I

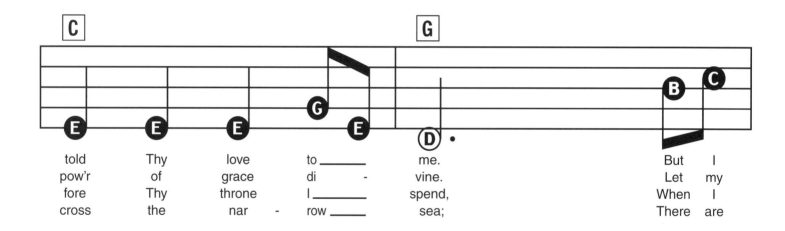

told Thy love to _____ me. But I
pow'r of grace di - vine. Let my
fore Thy throne I _____ spend, When I
cross the nar - row _____ sea; There are

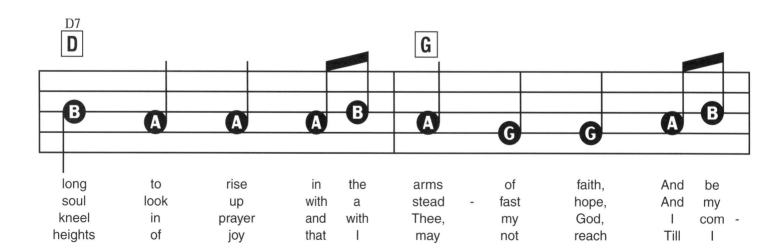

long to rise in the arms of faith, And be
soul look up with a stead - fast hope, And my
kneel in prayer and with Thee, my God, I com -
heights of joy that I may not reach Till I

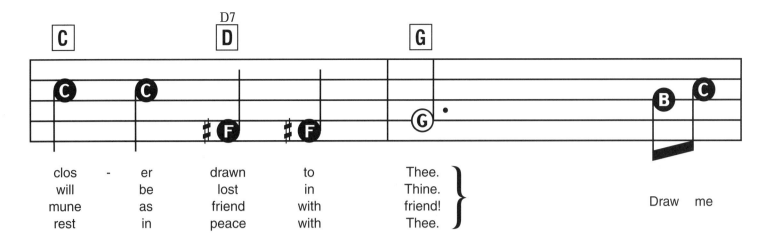

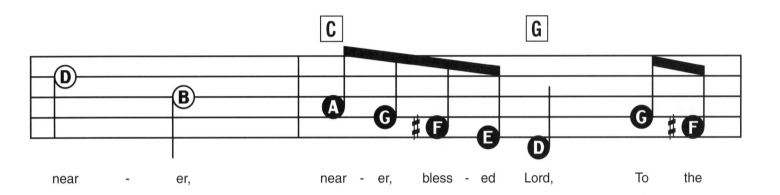

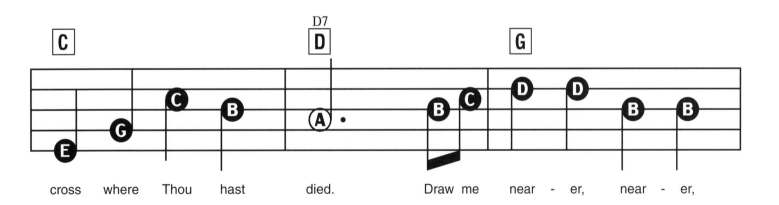

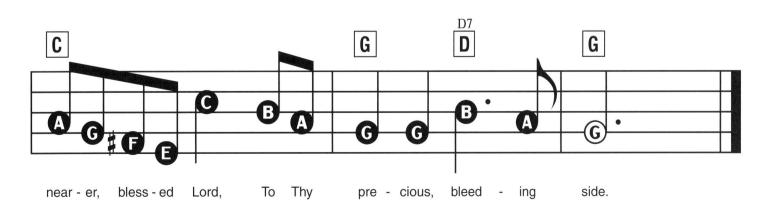

I Sing the Mighty Power of God

Registration 6
Rhythm: March

Words by Isaac Watts
Music from *Gesangbuch der Herzogl*

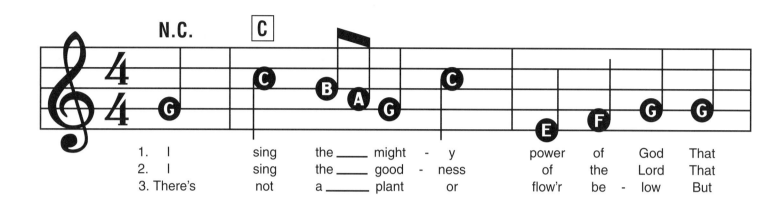

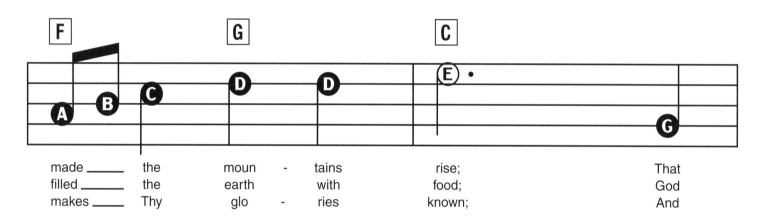

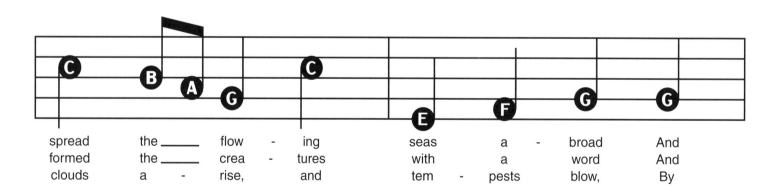

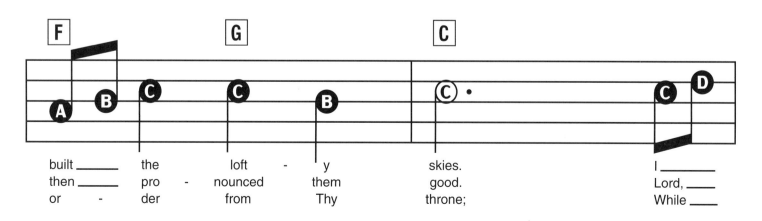

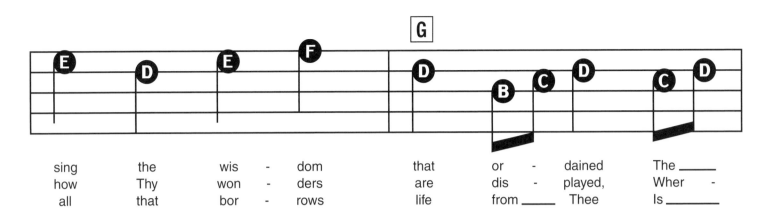

sing the wis - dom that or - dained The _____
how Thy won - ders are dis - played, Wher -
all that bor - rows life from _____ Thee Is _____

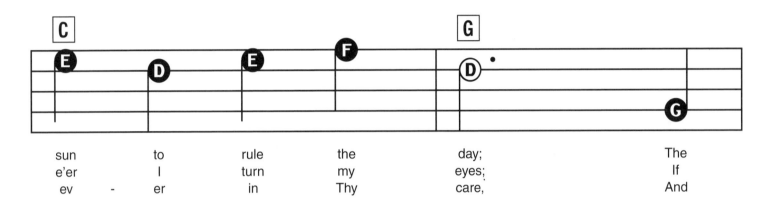

sun to rule the day; The
e'er I turn my eyes; If
ev - er in Thy care, And

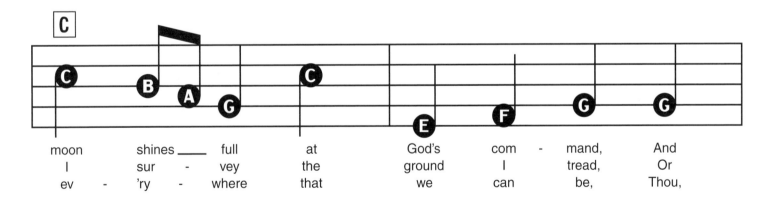

moon shines _____ full at God's com - mand, And
I sur - vey the ground I tread, Or
ev - 'ry - where that we can be, Thou,

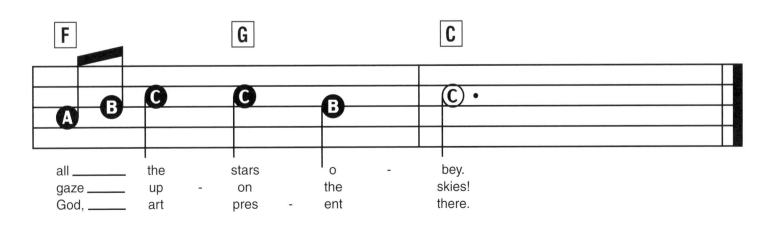

all _____ the stars o - bey.
gaze _____ up - on the skies!
God, _____ art pres - ent there.

I Surrender All

Registration 4
Rhythm: Fox Trot

Words by J.W. Van Deventer
Music by W.S. Weeden

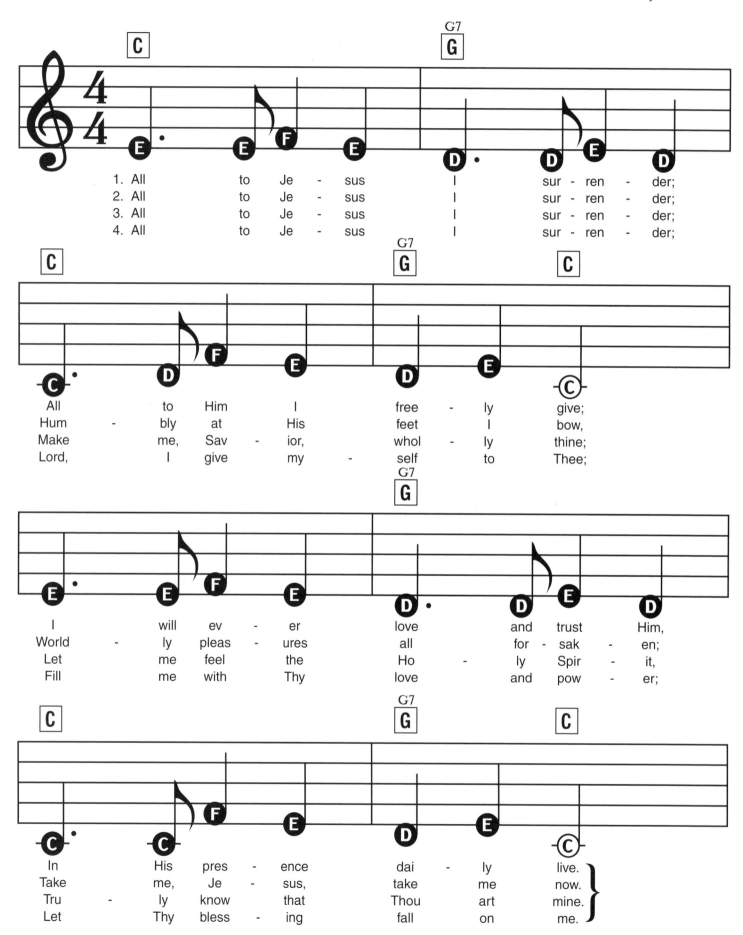

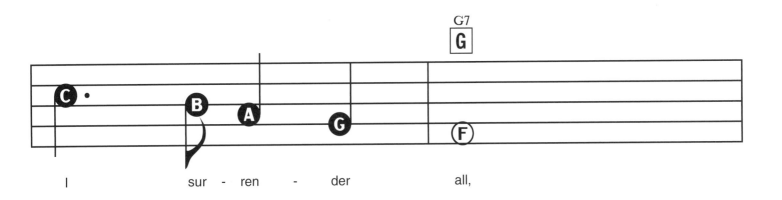

I sur - ren - der all,

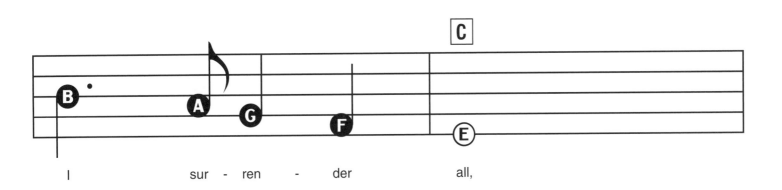

I sur - ren - der all,

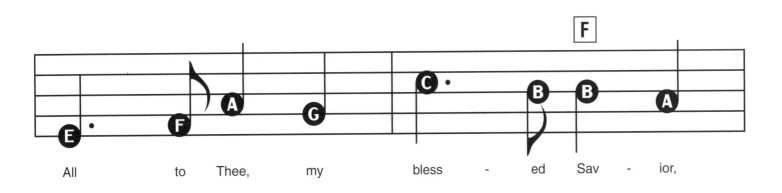

All to Thee, my bless - ed Sav - ior,

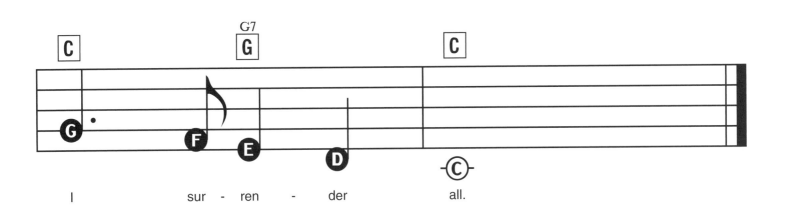

I sur - ren - der all.

Jesus, Keep Me Near the Cross

Registration 6
Rhythm: Waltz

Words by Fanny J. Crosby
Music by William H. Doane

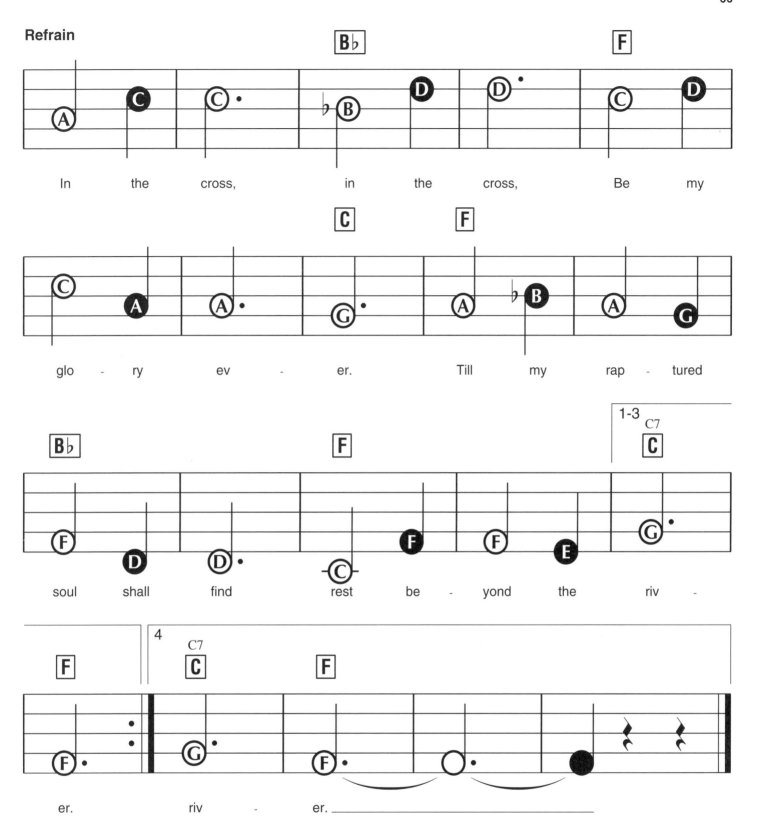

Additional Verses

3. Near the cross! O Lamb of God,
   Bring its scenes before me;
   Help me walk from day to day,
   With its shadows o'er me.
   Refrain

4. Near the cross I'll watch and wait,
   Hoping, trusting ever,
   Till I reach the golden strand,
   Just beyond the river.
   Refrain

Jesus Shall Reign

Registration 2
Rhythm: Fox Trot

Words by Isaac Watts
Music by John Hatton

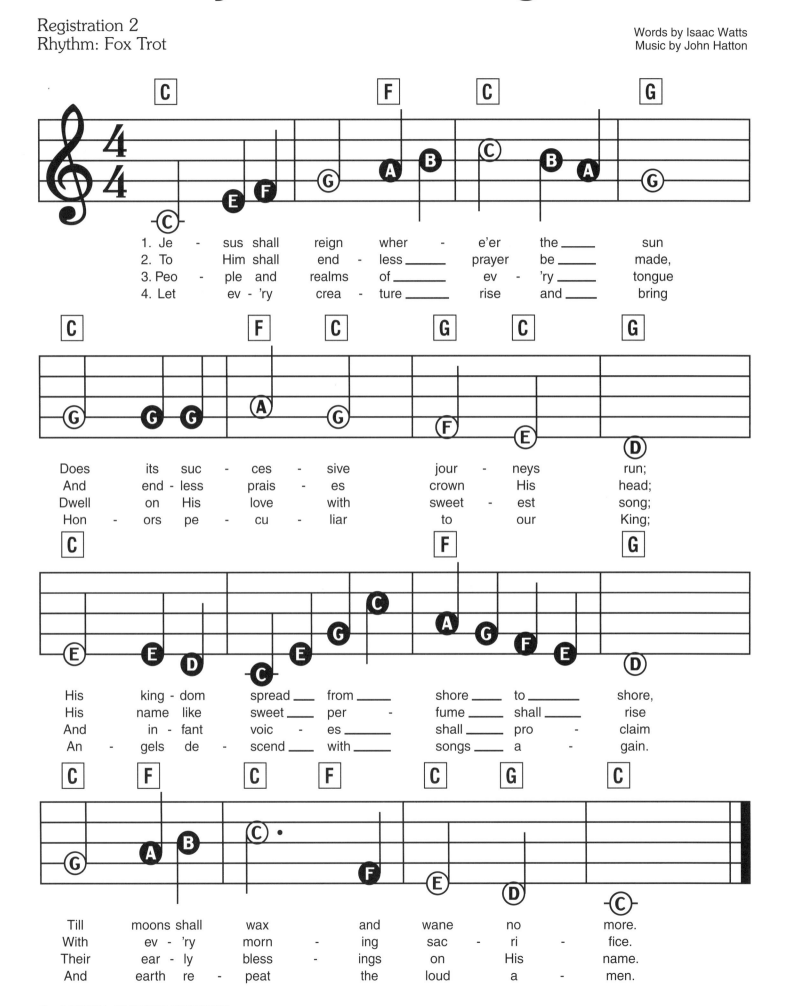

O Worship the King

Words by Robert Grant
Music attributed to Johann Michael Haydn
Arranged by William Gardiner

Registration 1
Rhythm: Waltz

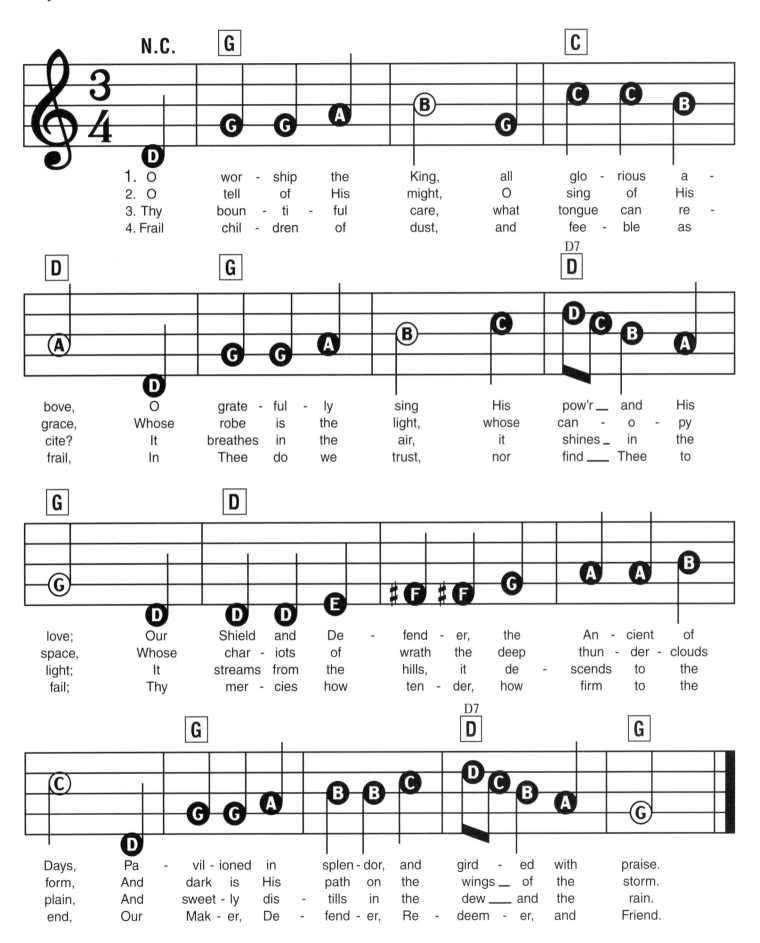

Joyful, Joyful, We Adore Thee

Registration 7
Rhythm: March

Words by Henry van Dyke
Music by Ludwig van Beethoven, melody from Ninth Symphony
Adapted by Edward Hodges

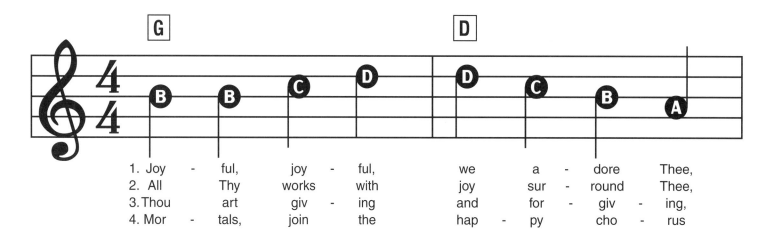

1. Joy - ful, joy - ful, we a - dore Thee,
2. All Thy works with joy sur - round Thee,
3. Thou art giv - ing and for - giv - ing,
4. Mor - tals, join the hap - py cho - rus

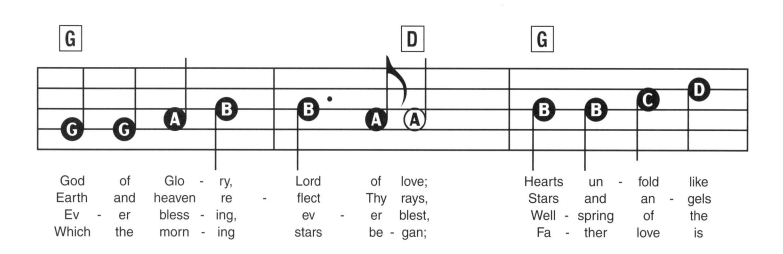

God of Glo - ry, Lord of love; Hearts un - fold like
Earth and heaven re - flect Thy rays, Stars and an - gels
Ev - er bless - ing, ev - er blest, Well - spring of the
Which the morn - ing stars be - gan; Fa - ther love is

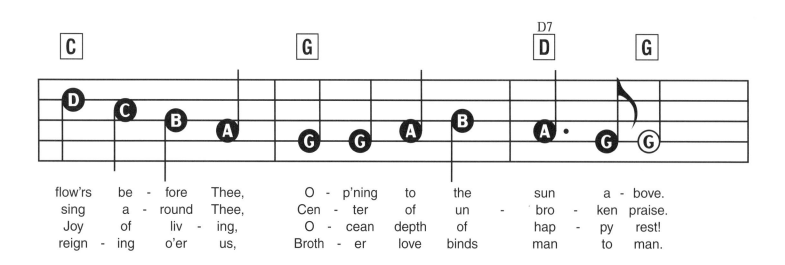

flow'rs be - fore Thee, O - p'ning to the sun a - bove.
sing a - round Thee, Cen - ter of un - bro - ken praise.
Joy of liv - ing, O - cean depth of hap - py rest!
reign - ing o'er us, Broth - er love binds man to man.

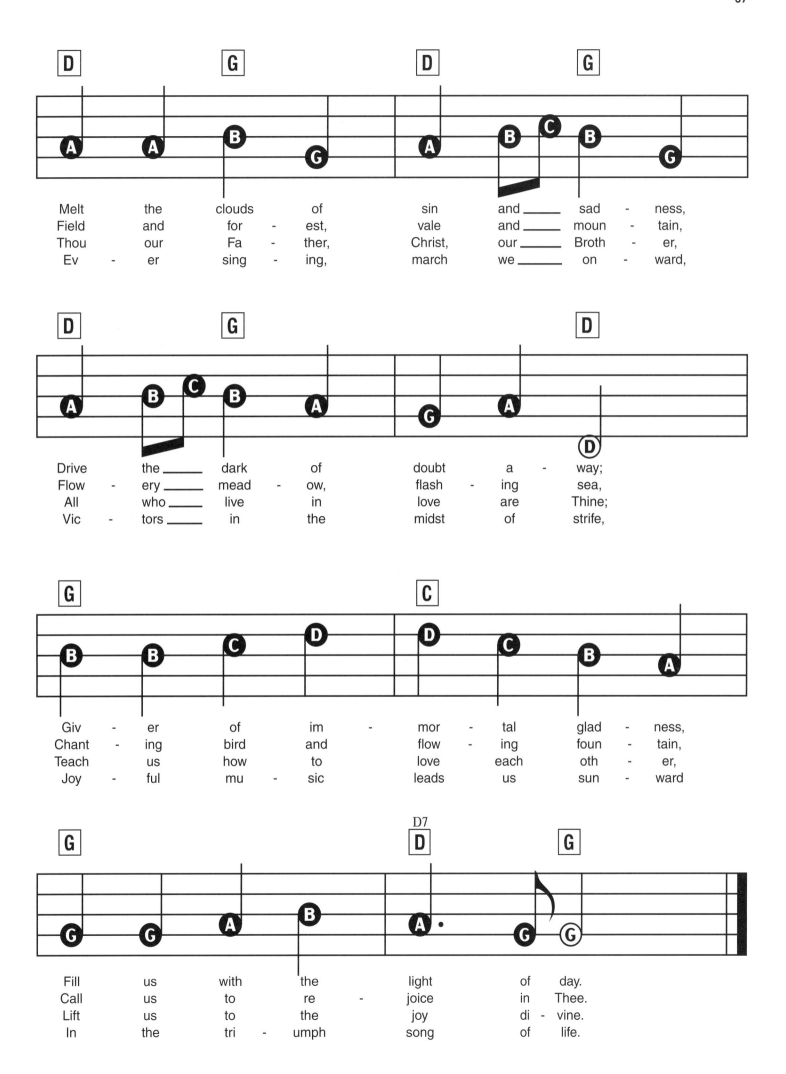

Just As I Am

Registration 1
Rhythm: Waltz

Words by Charlotte Elliott
Music by William B. Bradbury

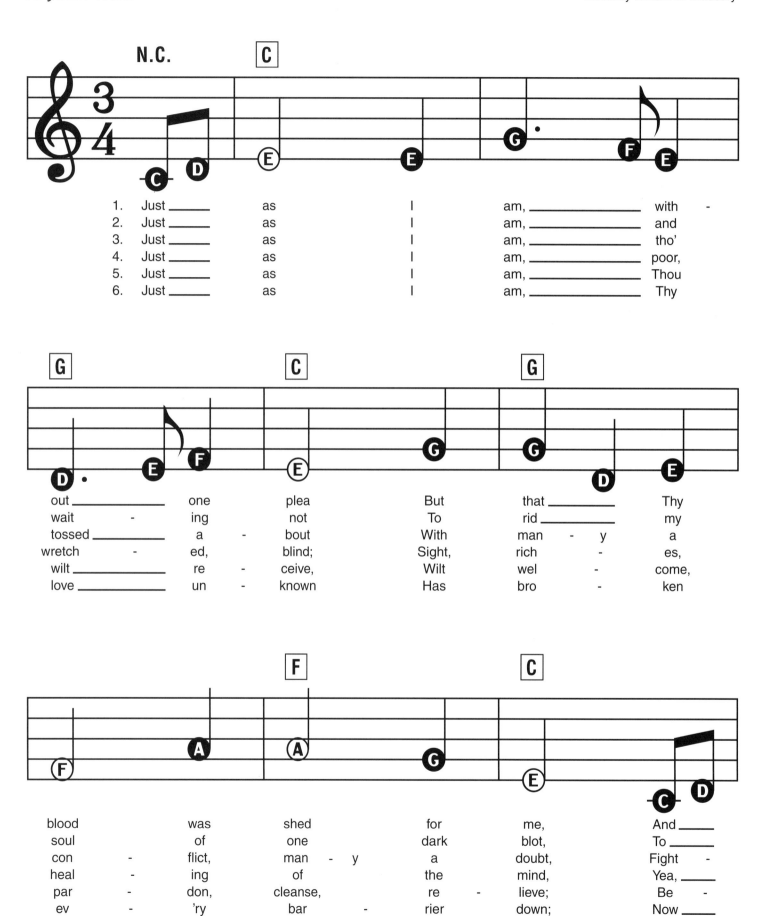

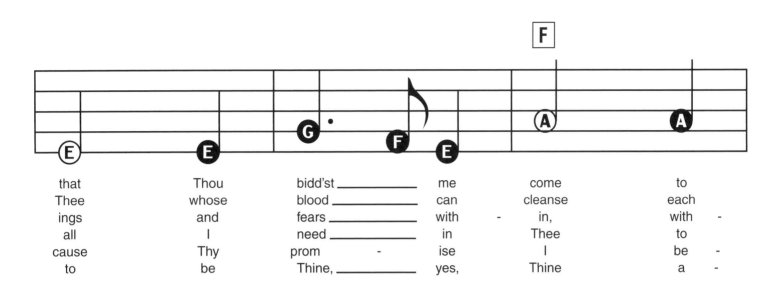

that	Thou	bidd'st _____	me	come	to
Thee	whose	blood _____	can	cleanse	each
ings	and	fears _____	with -	in,	with -
all	I	need _____	in	Thee	to
cause	Thy	prom -	ise	I	be -
to	be	Thine, _____	yes,	Thine	a -

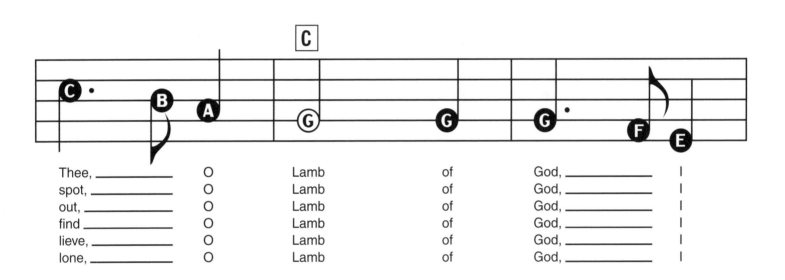

Thee, _____	O	Lamb	of	God, _____	I
spot, _____	O	Lamb	of	God, _____	I
out, _____	O	Lamb	of	God, _____	I
find _____	O	Lamb	of	God, _____	I
lieve, _____	O	Lamb	of	God, _____	I
lone, _____	O	Lamb	of	God, _____	I

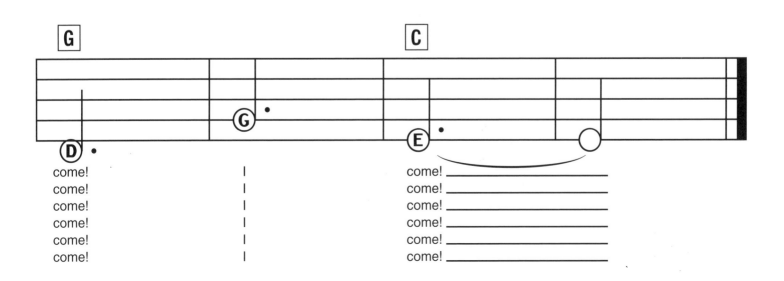

come!	I	come! _____
come!	I	come! _____
come!	I	come! _____
come!	I	come! _____
come!	I	come! _____
come!	I	come! _____

Leaning on the Everlasting Arms

Registration 7
Rhythm: March

Words by Elisha A. Hoffman
Music by Anthony J. Showalter

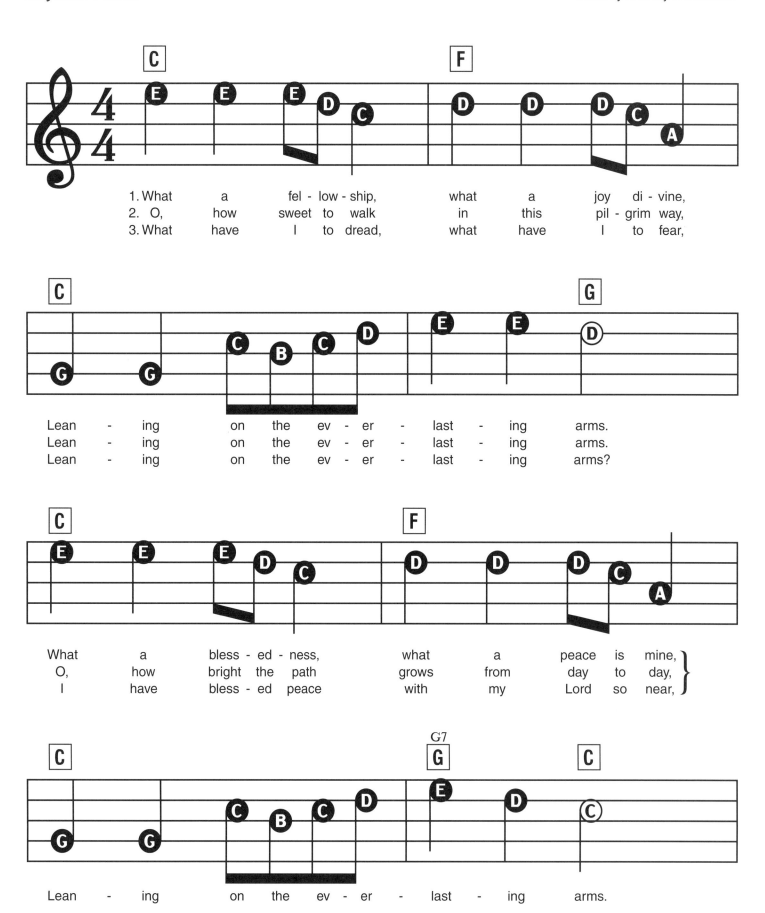

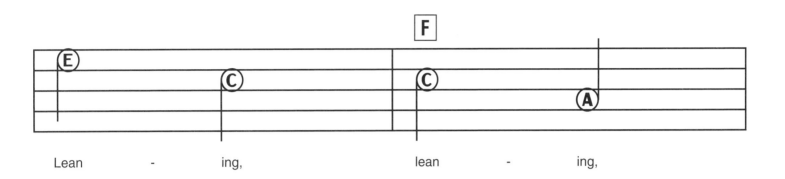

Lean - ing,   lean - ing,

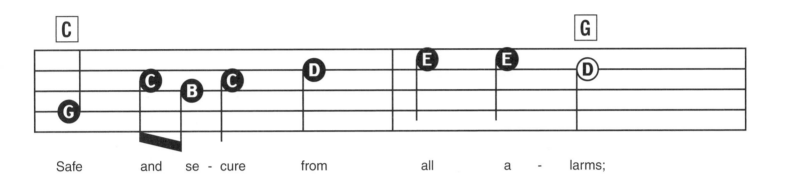

Safe   and   se - cure   from   all   a - larms;

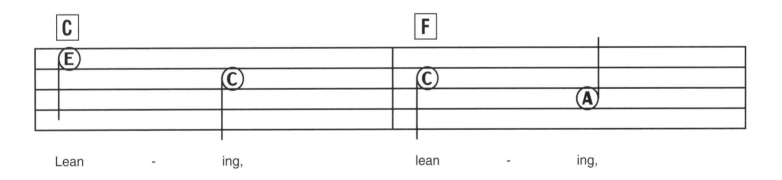

Lean - ing,   lean - ing,

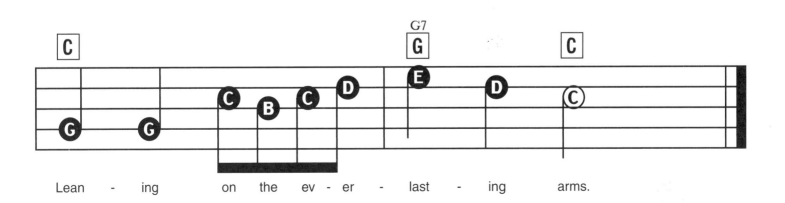

Lean - ing   on the ev - er - last - ing   arms.

My Jesus, I Love Thee

Registration 1
Rhythm: Fox Trot

Words by William R. Featherstone
Music by Adoniram J. Gordon

1. My Je - sus, I love _____ Thee, I
2. I love Thee be - cause _____ Thou hast
3. I'll love Thee in life, _____ Thou will
4. In man - sions of glo - ry and

know Thou art mine; For
first lov - ed me, And
love Thee in death, And
end - less de - light, I'll

Thee all the fol - lies of
pur - chased my par - don on
praise Thee as long _____ as Thou
ev - er a - dore _____ Thee in

sin I re - sign; My
Cal - va - ry's tree; I
lend - est me breath; And
heav - en so bright; I'll

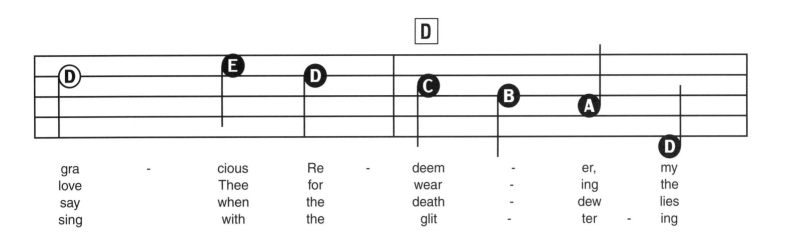

gra	-	cious	Re	-	deem	-	er,	my
love		Thee	for		wear	-	ing	the
say		when	the		death	-	dew	lies
sing		with	the		glit	-	ter	-	ing

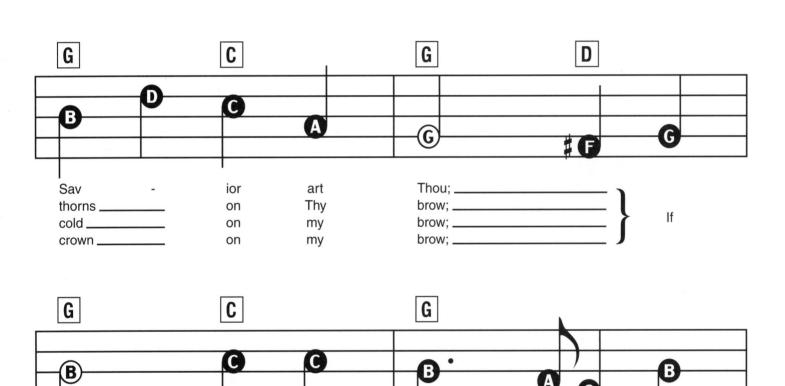

Sav	-	ior	art	Thou; _____	
thorns _____		on	Thy	brow; _____	}	If
cold _____		on	my	brow; _____	
crown _____		on	my	brow; _____	

| ev | - | er | I | loved _____ Thee, | my |

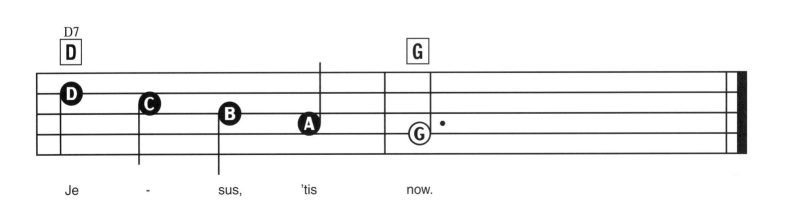

| Je | - | sus, | 'tis | now. |

Near to the Heart of God

Registration 2
Rhythm: Fox Trot

Words and Music by
Cleland B. McAfee

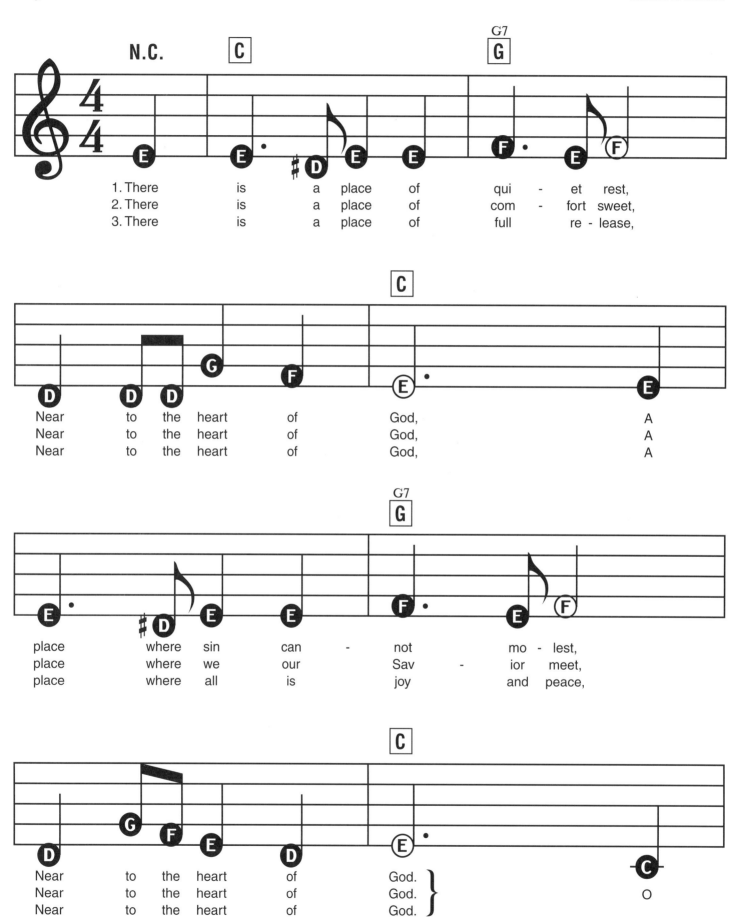

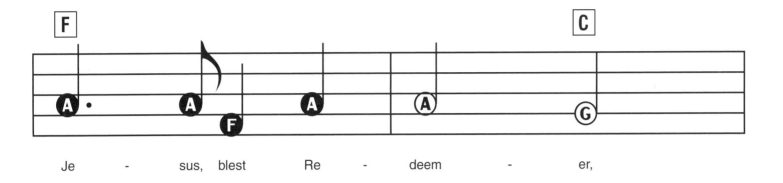

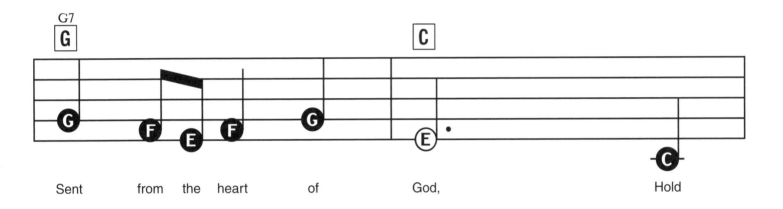

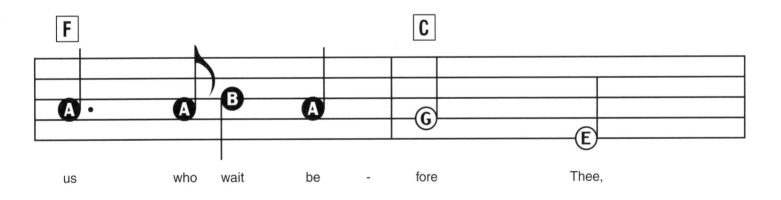

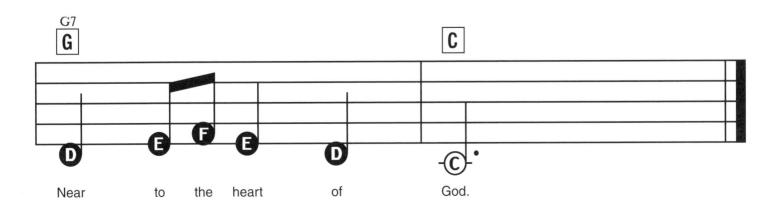

Nearer, My God, to Thee

Registration 3
Rhythm: Fox Trot

Words by Sarah F. Adams
Based on Genesis 28:10-22
Music by Lowell Mason

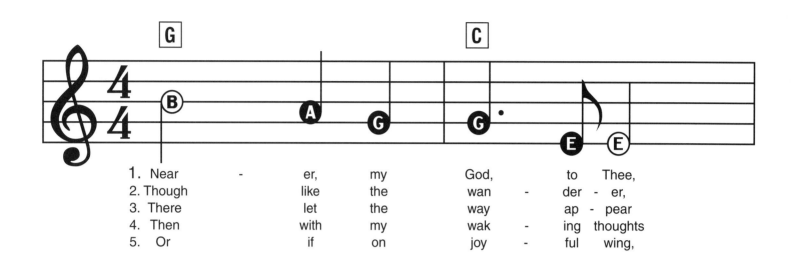

1. Near - er, my God, to Thee,
2. Though like the wan - der - er,
3. There let the way ap - pear
4. Then with my wak - ing thoughts
5. Or if on joy - ful wing,

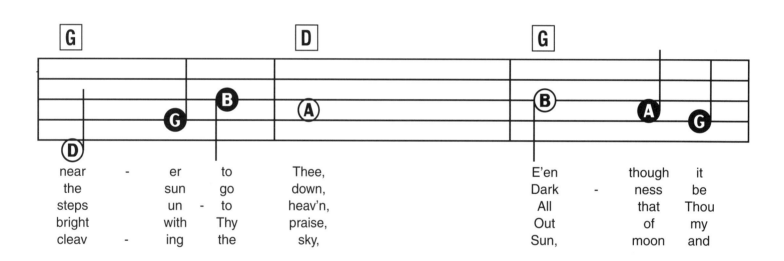

near - er to Thee, E'en though it
the sun go down, Dark - ness be
steps un - to heav'n, All that Thou
bright with Thy praise, Out of my
cleav - ing the sky, Sun, moon and

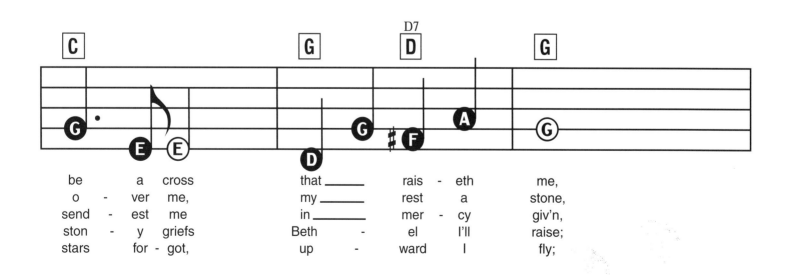

be a cross that _____ rais - eth me,
o - ver me, my _____ rest a stone,
send - est me in _____ mer - cy giv'n,
ston - y griefs Beth - el I'll raise;
stars for - got, up - ward I fly;

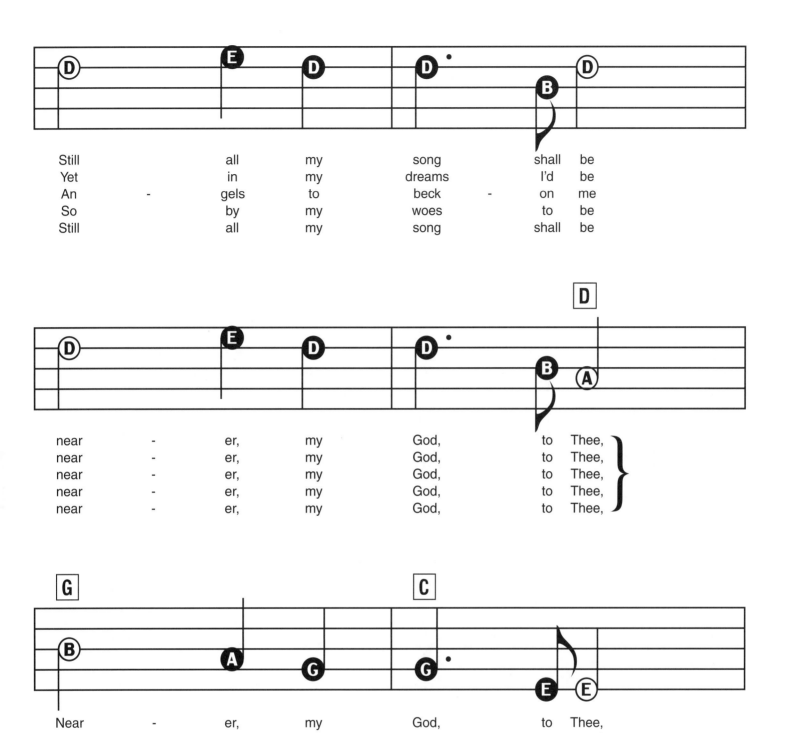

Still   all   my   song   shall be
Yet   in   my   dreams   I'd be
An - gels   to   beck - on me
So   by   my   woes   to be
Still   all   my   song   shall be

near - er,   my   God,   to Thee,
near - er,   my   God,   to Thee,
near - er,   my   God,   to Thee,
near - er,   my   God,   to Thee,
near - er,   my   God,   to Thee,

Near - er,   my   God,   to Thee,

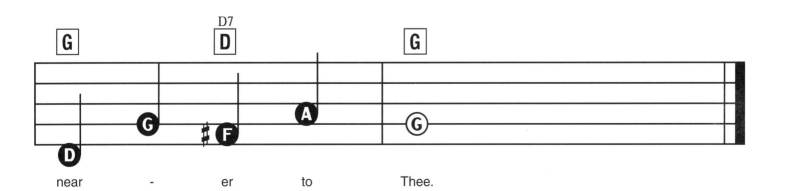

near - er to Thee.

Only Trust Him

Registration 2
Rhythm: Fox Trot

Words and Music by
John H. Stockton

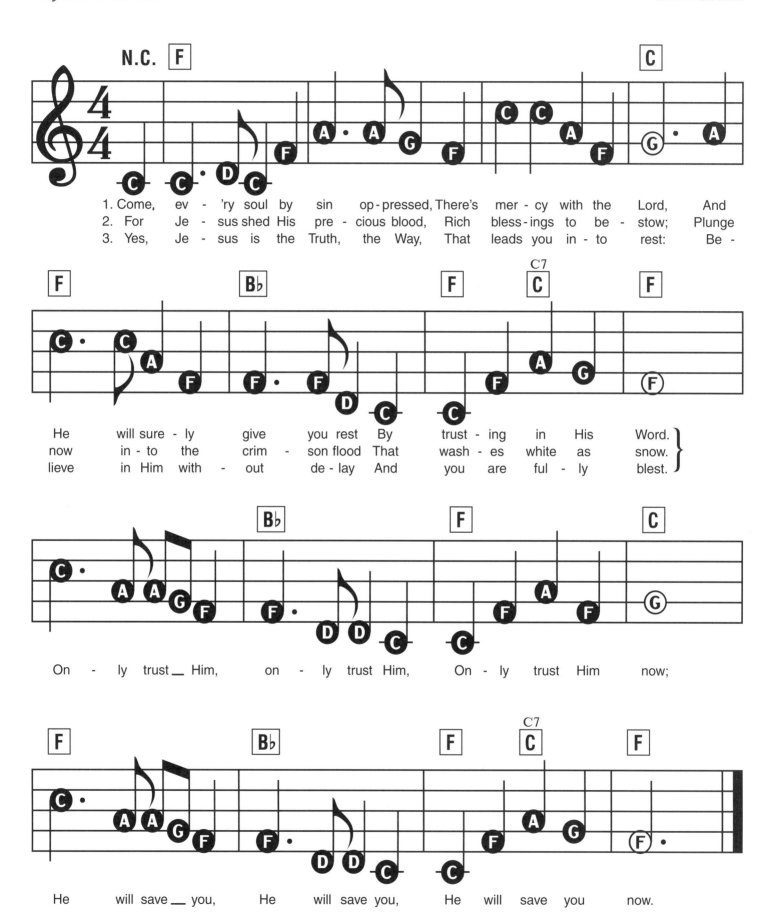

1. Come, ev - 'ry soul by sin op - pressed, There's mer - cy with the Lord, And
2. For Je - sus shed His pre - cious blood, Rich bless - ings to be - stow; And Plunge
3. Yes, Je - sus is the Truth, the Way, That leads you in - to rest: Be -

He will sure - ly give you rest By trust - ing in His Word.
now in - to the crim - son flood That wash - es white as snow.
lieve in Him with - out de - lay And you are ful - ly blest.

On - ly trust Him, on - ly trust Him, On - ly trust Him now;

He will save you, He will save you, He will save you now.

Praise to the Lord, the Almighty

Registration 2
Rhythm: Waltz

Words by Joachim Neander
Translated by Catherine Winkworth
Music from *Erneuerten Gesangbuch*

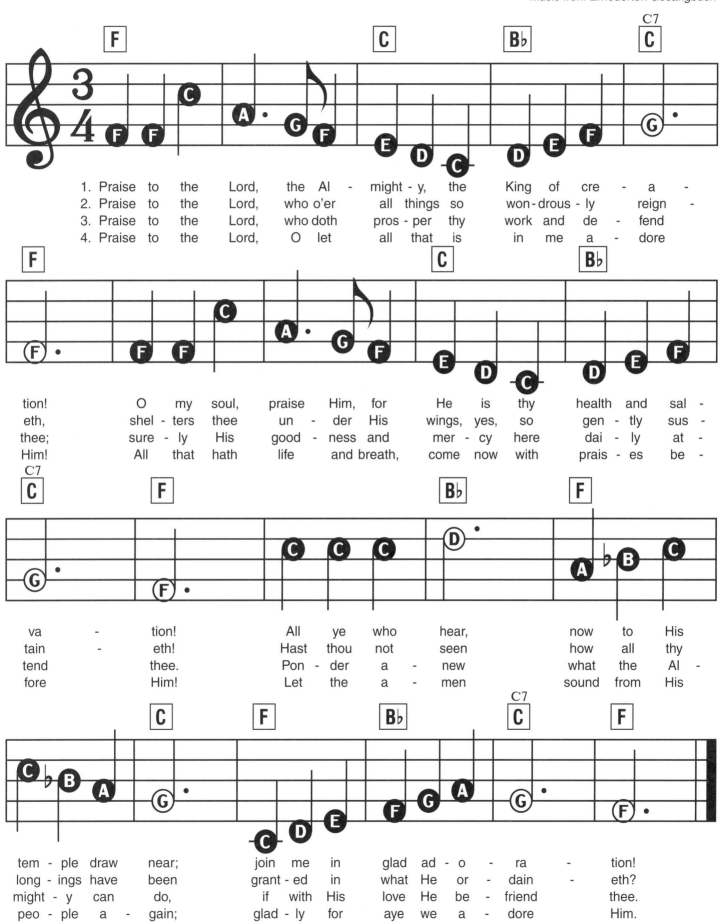

Savior, Like a Shepherd Lead Us

Registration 3
Rhythm: Fox Trot

Words from *Hymns for the Young*
Attributed to Dorothy A. Thrupp
Music by William B. Bradbury

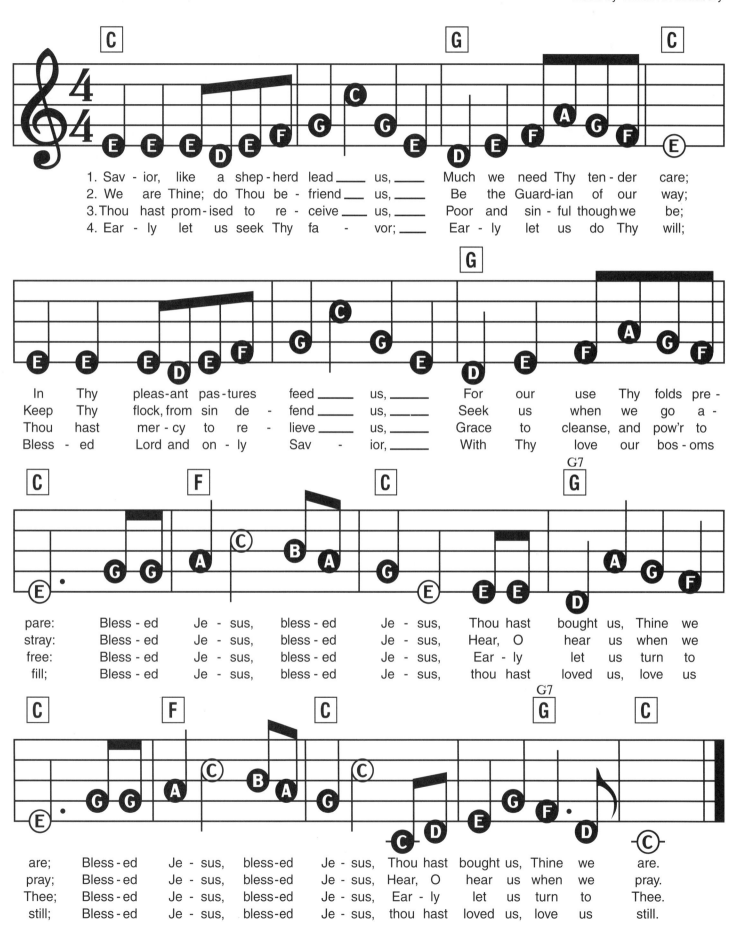

Stand Up, Stand Up for Jesus

Registration 7
Rhythm: March

Words by George Duffield, Jr.
Music by George J. Webb

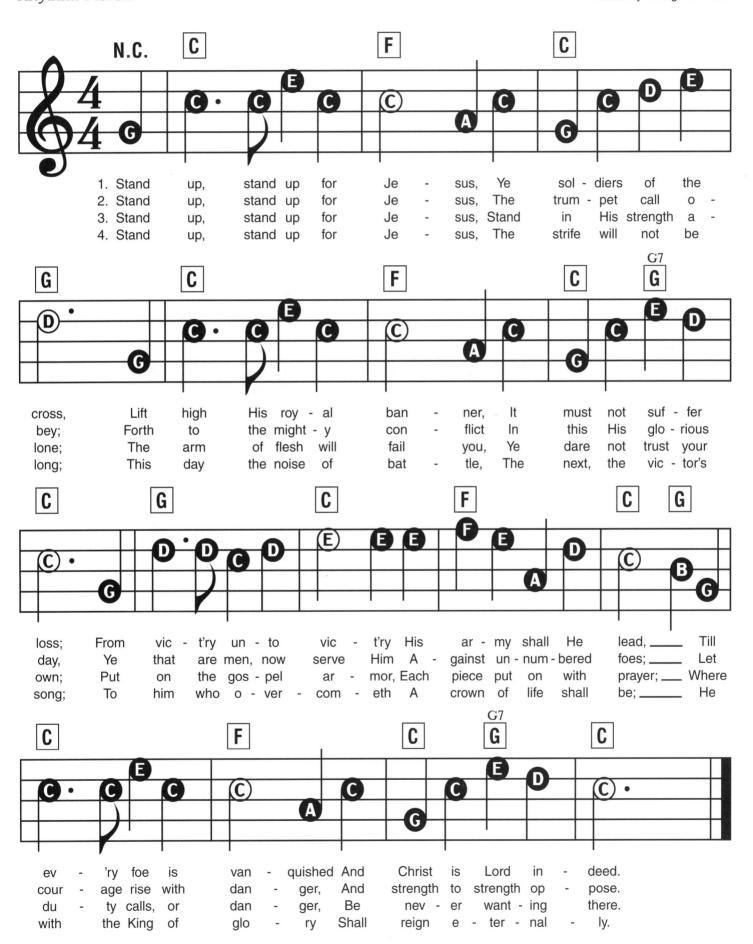

Standing on the Promises

Registration 5
Rhythm: March or Swing

Words and Music by
R. Kelso Carter

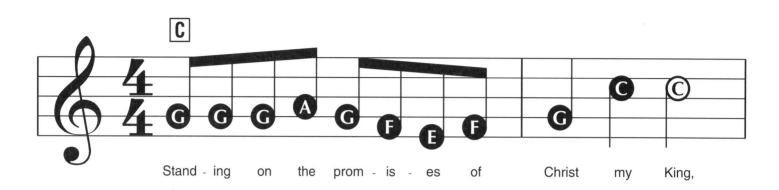

Stand - ing on the prom - is - es of Christ my King,

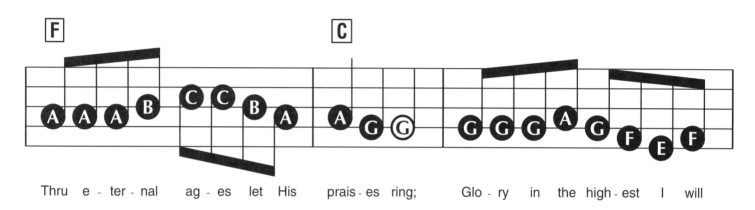

Thru e - ter - nal ag - es let His prais - es ring; Glo - ry in the high - est I will

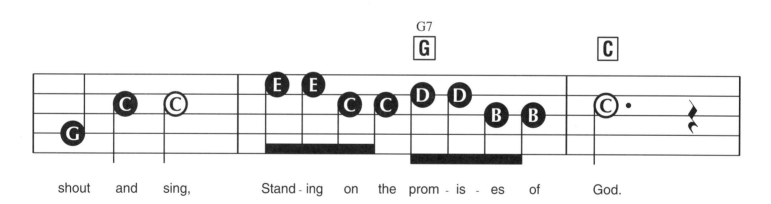

shout and sing, Stand - ing on the prom - is - es of God.

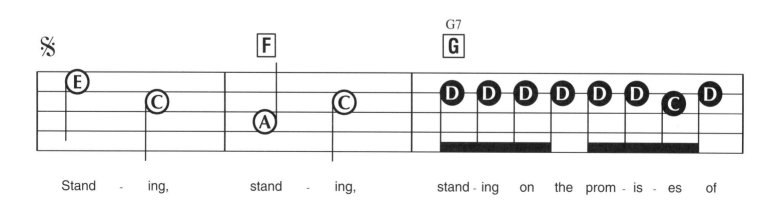

Stand - ing, stand - ing, stand - ing on the prom - is - es of

53

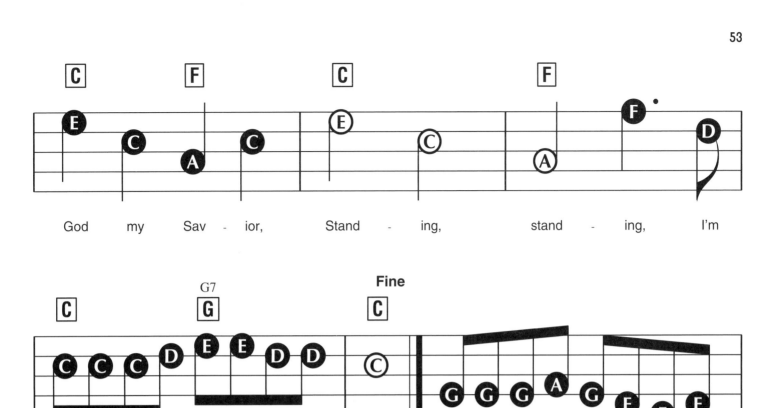

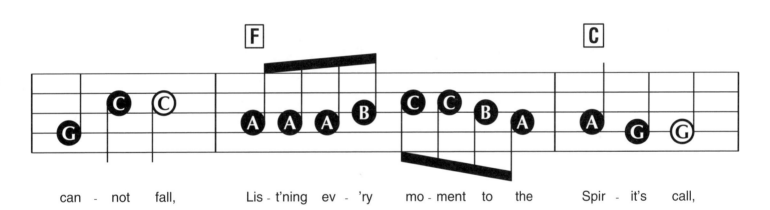

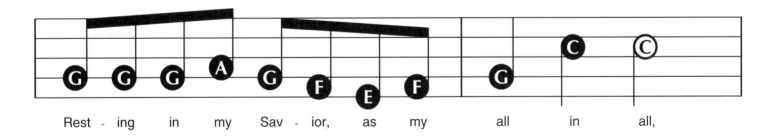

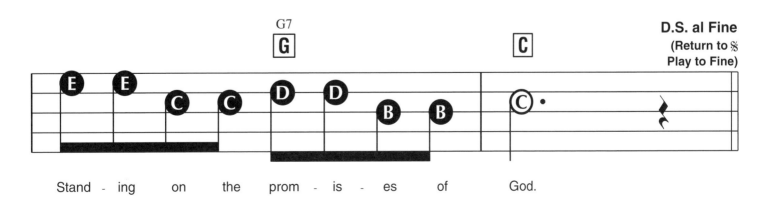

Sweet Hour of Prayer

Registration 2
Rhythm: 6/8 March

Words by William W. Walford
Music by William B. Bradbury

1. Sweet hour of prayer, sweet hour of prayer, That
2. Sweet hour of prayer, sweet hour of prayer, Thy
3. Sweet hour of prayer, sweet hour of prayer, Thy
4. Sweet hour of prayer, sweet hour of prayer, May

calls me from a world of care, And
joy I feel, the bliss I share Of
wings shall my pe - ti - tion bear To
I thy con - so - la - tion share, Till

bids me at my Fa - ther's throne Make
those whose anx - ious spir - its burn With
Him whose truth and faith - ful - ness En -
from Mount Pis - gah's loft - y height I

all my wants and wish - es known. In
strong de - sire for thy re - turn. With
gage the wait - ing soul to bless. And
view my home and take my flight. This

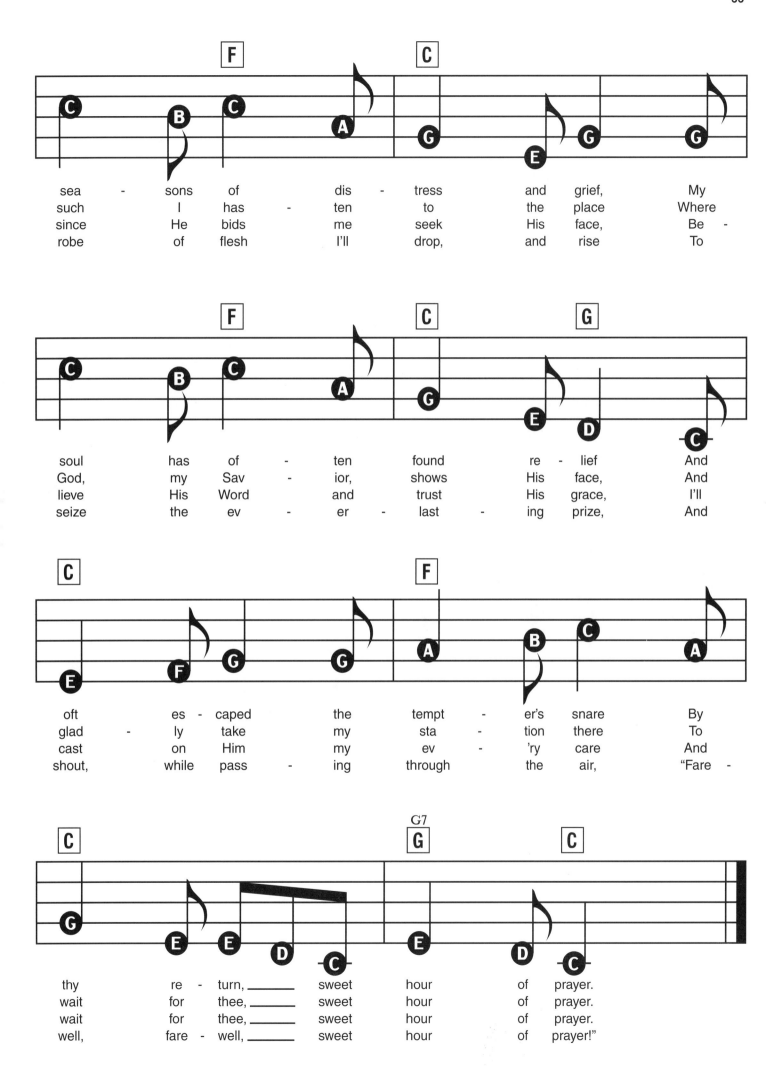

This Is My Father's World

Registration 8
Rhythm: Ballad or Country

Words by Maltbie D. Babcock
Music by Franklin L. Sheppard

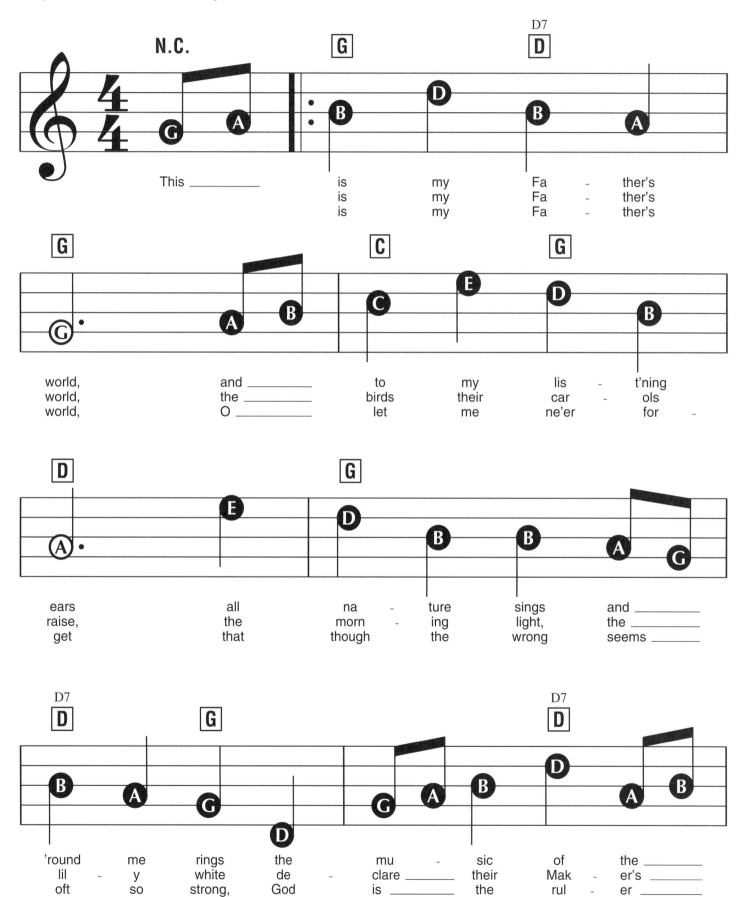

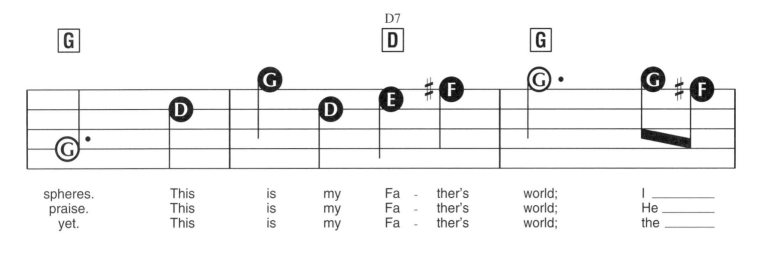

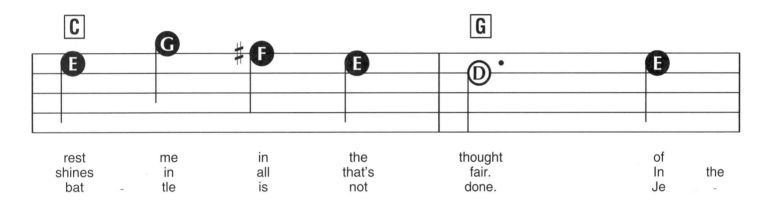

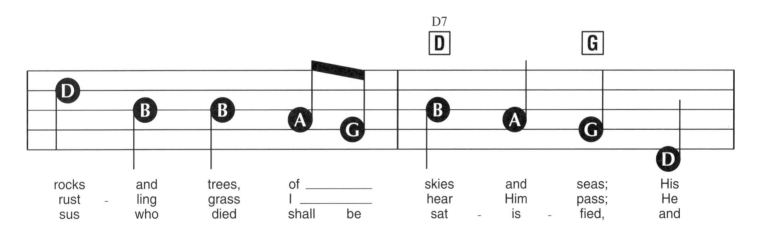

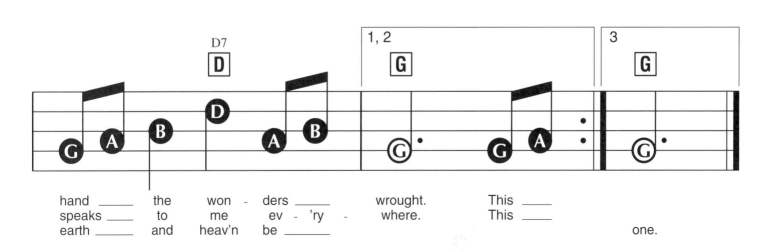

'Tis So Sweet to Trust in Jesus

Registration 1
Rhythm: Fox Trot

Words by Louisa M.R. Stead
Music by William J. Kirkpatrick

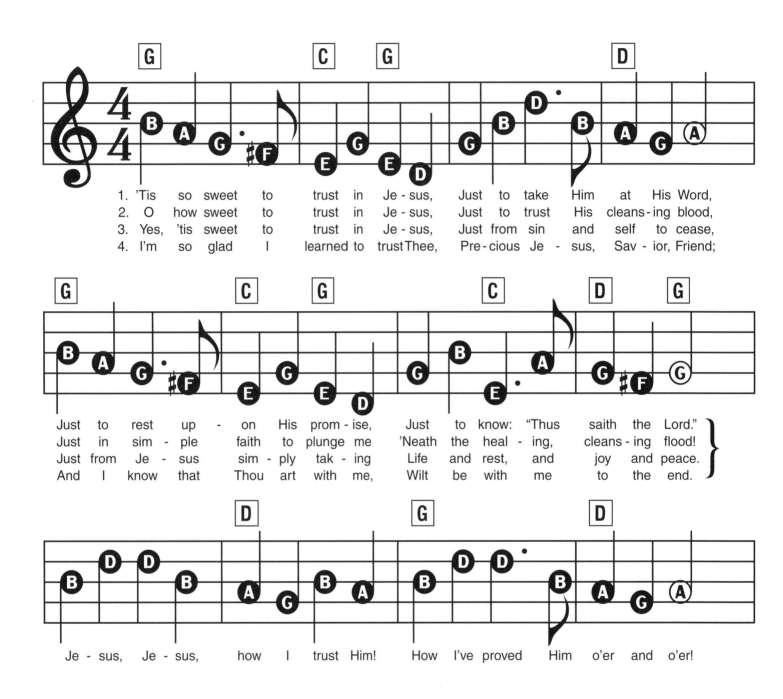

1. 'Tis so sweet to trust in Je - sus, Just to take Him at His Word,
2. O how sweet to trust in Je - sus, Just to trust His cleans - ing blood,
3. Yes, 'tis sweet to trust in Je - sus, Just from sin and self to cease,
4. I'm so glad I learned to trust Thee, Pre - cious Je - sus, Sav - ior, Friend;

Just to rest up - on His prom - ise, Just to know: "Thus saith the Lord."
Just in sim - ple faith to plunge me 'Neath the heal - ing, cleans - ing flood!
Just from Je - sus sim - ply tak - ing Life and rest, and joy and peace.
And I know that Thou art with me, Wilt be with me to the end.

Je - sus, Je - sus, how I trust Him! How I've proved Him o'er and o'er!

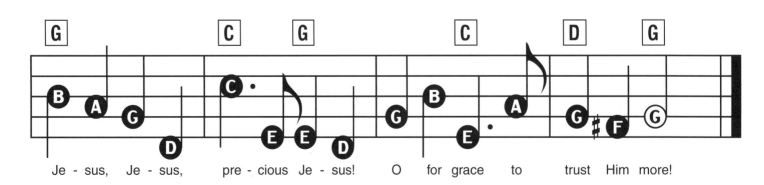

Je - sus, Je - sus, pre - cious Je - sus! O for grace to trust Him more!

What a Friend We Have in Jesus

Registration 8
Rhythm: Fox Trot

Words by Joseph M. Scriven
Music by Charles C. Converse

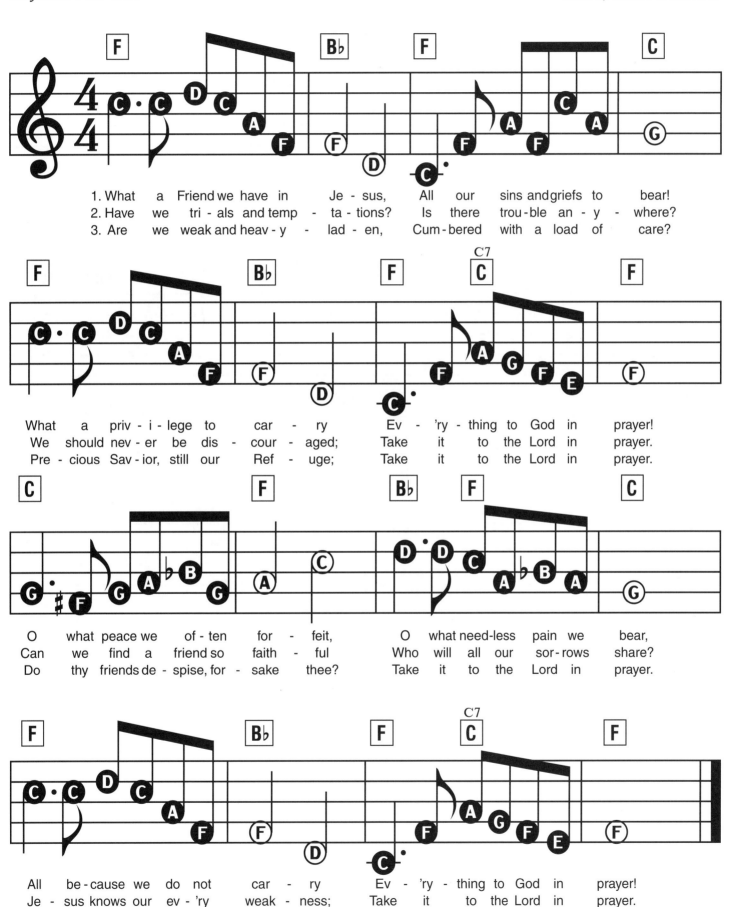

Wonderful Words of Life

Registration 2
Rhythm: 6/8 March

Words and Music by
Philip P. Bliss

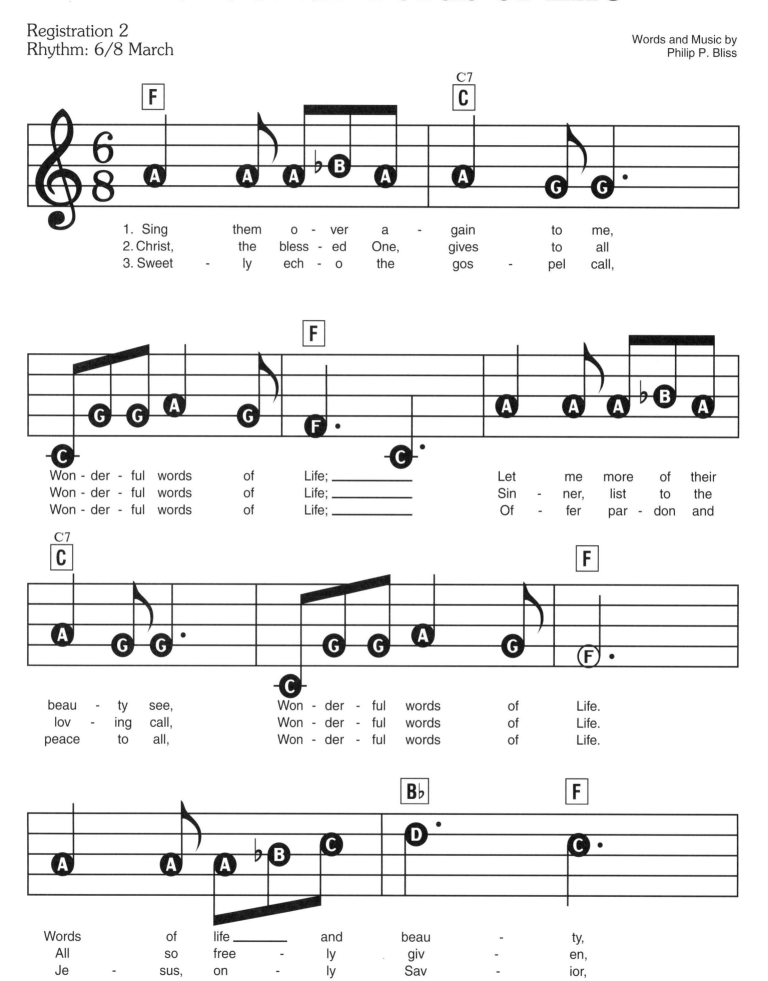

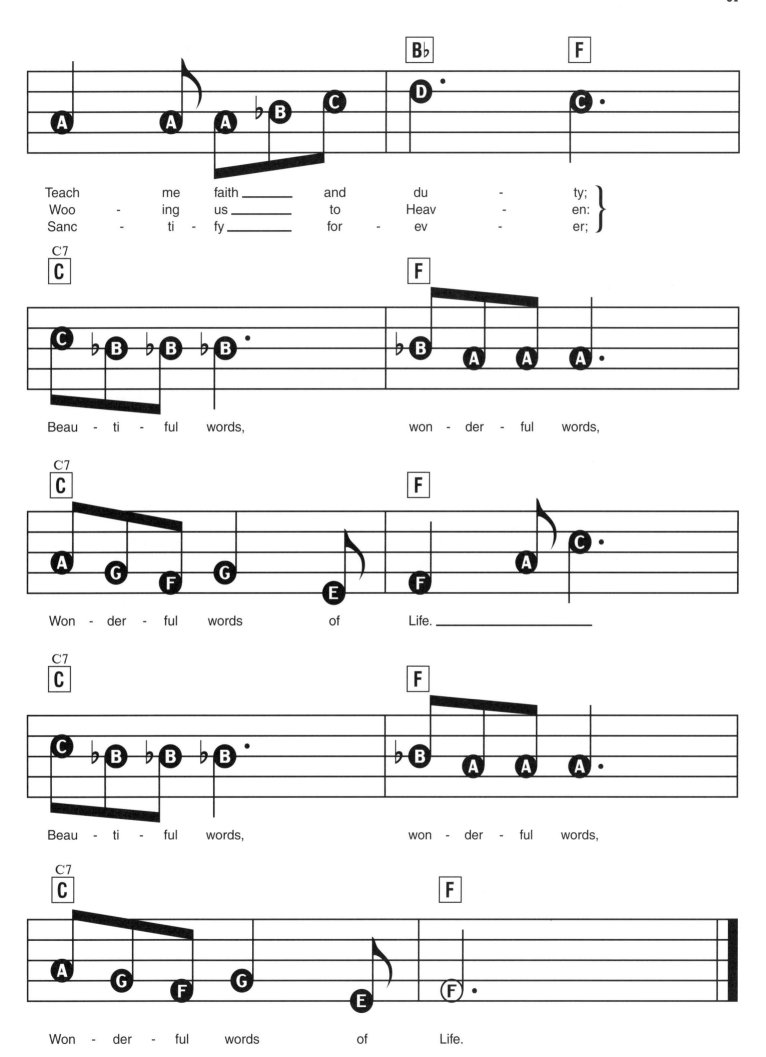

When I Survey the Wondrous Cross

Registration 3
Rhythm: Fox Trot

Words by Isaac Watts
Music arranged by Lowell Mason
Based on Plainsong

Registration Guide

- Match the Registration number on the song to the corresponding numbered category below. Select and activate an instrumental sound available on your instrument.

- Choose an automatic rhythm appropriate to the mood and style of the song. (Consult your Owner's Guide for proper operation of automatic rhythm features.)

- Adjust the tempo and volume controls to comfortable settings.

Registration

1	Mellow	Flutes, Clarinet, Oboe, Flugel Horn, Trombone, French Horn, Organ Flutes
2	Ensemble	Brass Section, Sax Section, Wind Ensemble, Full Organ, Theater Organ
3	Strings	Violin, Viola, Cello, Fiddle, String Ensemble, Pizzicato, Organ Strings
4	Guitars	Acoustic/Electric Guitars, Banjo, Mandolin, Dulcimer, Ukulele, Hawaiian Guitar
5	Mallets	Vibraphone, Marimba, Xylophone, Steel Drums, Bells, Celesta, Chimes
6	Liturgical	Pipe Organ, Hand Bells, Vocal Ensemble, Choir, Organ Flutes
7	Bright	Saxophones, Trumpet, Mute Trumpet, Synth Leads, Jazz/Gospel Organs
8	Piano	Piano, Electric Piano, Honky Tonk Piano, Harpsichord, Clavi
9	Novelty	Melodic Percussion, Wah Trumpet, Synth, Whistle, Kazoo, Perc. Organ
10	Bellows	Accordion, French Accordion, Mussette, Harmonica, Pump Organ, Bagpipes

FOR ORGANS, PIANOS & ELECTRONIC KEYBOARDS

E-Z PLAY® TODAY PUBLICATIONS

The E-Z Play® Today songbook series is the shortest distance between beginning music and playing fun
*Check out this list of highlights and visit **balleonard.com** for a complete listing of all volumes and songlists.*

00102278 **1. Favorite Songs with 3 Chords** $9.99
00100374 **2. Country Sound** $12.99
00284446 **3. Contemporary Disney**.$16.99
00100382 **4. Dance Band Greats**........$7.95
00100305 **5. All-Time Standards**......$10.99
00282553 **6. Songs of the Beatles**....$14.99
00100442 **7. Hits from Musicals**........$8.99
00100490 **8. Patriotic Songs**.............$8.99
00236235 **9. Christmas Time**............$9.99
00198012 **10. Songs of Hawaii**..........$12.99
00137580 **11. 75 Light Classical Songs**.$19.99
00110284 **12. Star Wars**......................$10.99
00100248 **13. 3-Chord Country Songs**.$14.99
00100248 **14. All-Time Requests**..........$8.99
00241118 **15. Simple Songs**................$14.99
00266435 **16. Broadway's Best**...........$12.99
00100415 **17. Fireside Singalong**........$14.99
00149113 **18. 30 Classical Masterworks**.$8.99
00137780 **19. Top Country Songs**.......$12.99
00102277 **20. Hymns**...........................$9.99
00197200 **21. Good Ol' Gospel**...........$12.99
00100570 **22. Sacred Sounds**..............$8.99
00234685 **23. First 50 Songs You Should Play on Keyboard**........$16.99
00249679 **24. Songs with 3 Chords**....$14.99
00140724 **25. Happy Birthday to You & Other Great Songs**...$10.99
14041364 **26. Bob Dylan**....................$12.99
00001236 **27. 60 of the Easiest to Play Songs with 3 Chords**.....$9.99
00101598 **28. 50 Classical Themes**......$9.99
00100135 **29. Love Songs**....................$9.99
00100030 **30. Country Connection**.....$12.99
00100010 **31. Big Band Favorites**........$9.99
00249578 **32. Songs with 4 Chords**....$14.99
00160720 **33. Ragtime Classics**...........$9.99
00100122 **36. Good Ol' Songs**............$12.99
00100410 **37. Favorite Latin Songs**......$8.99
00156394 **38. Best of Adele**...............$10.99
00159567 **39. Best Children's Songs Ever**...............$17.99
00119955 **40. Coldplay**......................$10.99
00287762 **41. Bohemian Rhapsody**....$14.99
00100123 **42. Baby Boomers Songbook**.$10.99
00102135 **44. Best of Willie Nelson**..$14.99
00100460 **45. Love Ballads**.................$8.99
00156236 **46. 15 Chart Hits**...............$12.99
00100007 **47. Duke Ellington**..............$8.95
00100343 **48. Gospel Songs of Johnny Cash**...............$9.99
00236314 **49. Beauty and the Beast**...$12.99
00102114 **50. Best of Patsy Cline** $9.99
00100208 **51. Essential Songs: 1950s**$17.99
00100209 **52. Essential Songs: 1960s**$19.99
00348318 **53. 100 Most Beautiful Christmas Songs** $22.99
00199268 **54. Acoustic Songs**............$12.99
00100342 **55. Johnny Cash**.................$12.99
00137703 **56. Jersey Boys** $12.99
00100118 **57. More of the Best Songs Ever**...............$19.99
00100285 **58. Four-Chord Songs**.......$10.99
00100353 **59. Christmas Songs**..........$10.99
00100304 **60. Songs for All Occasions**.$16.99
00100409 **62. Favorite Hymns**............$7.99
00278397 **63. Classical Music**.............$7.99
00100223 **64. Wicked**.........................$12.99
00100217 **65. Hymns with 3 Chords**...$8.99
00232258 **66. La La Land**...................$12.99
00100268 **68. Pirates of the Caribbean**.$12.99
00100449 **69. It's Gospel**....................$9.99
00100432 **70. Gospel Greats**...............$8.99
00236744 **71. 21 Top Hits**..................$12.99
00100117 **72. Canciones Románticas**.$10.99
00237558 **73. Michael Jackson**............$12.99
00147049 **74. Over the Rainbow & 40 More Great Songs** ..$12.99
00100568 **75. Sacred Moments**...........$6.95
00100572 **76. The Sound of Music**......$10.99

00238941 **77. Andrew Lloyd Webber**....$12.99
00100530 **78. Oklahoma!**....................$6.95
00248709 **79. Roadhouse Country**....$12.99
00100200 **80. Essential Paul Anka**.......$8.95
00100262 **82. Big Book of Folk Pop Rock**...............$14.99
00100584 **83. Swingtime**......................$7.95
00265416 **84. Ed Sheeran**...................$14.99
00100221 **85. Cowboy Songs**...............$7.95
00265488 **86. Leonard Cohen**............$12.99
00100286 **87. 50 Worship Standards**..$14.99
00100287 **88. Glee**...............................$9.99
00100577 **89. Songs for Children**.......$9.99
00290104 **90. Elton John Anthology**..$16.99
00100034 **91. 30 Songs for a Better World**...............$10.99
00100288 **92. Michael Bublé Crazy Love**$10.99
00100036 **93. Country Hits**.................$12.99
00100219 **95. Phantom of the Opera**.$12.99
00100263 **96. Mamma Mia**..................$10.99
00102317 **97. Elvis Presley**.................$14.99
00109768 **98. Flower Power**................$16.99
00275360 **99. The Greatest Showman**.$12.99
00282486 **100. The New Standards**.....$19.99
00100000 **101. Annie**...........................$10.99
00286388 **102. Dear Evan Hansen**......$12.99
00119237 **103. Two-Chord Songs**.........$9.99
00147057 **104. Hallelujah & 40 More Great Songs**..$14.99
00287417 **105. River Flows in You & Other Beautiful Songs**.$12.99
00139940 **106. 20 Top Hits**.................$14.99
00100256 **107. The Best Praise & Worship Songs Ever** $16.99
00100363 **108. Classical Themes**..........$7.99
00102232 **109. Motown's Greatest Hits** .$12.95
00101566 **110. Neil Diamond Collection** .$15.99
00100119 **111. Season's Greetings** $15.99
00101498 **112. Best of the Beatles** $21.99
00100134 **113. Country Gospel USA**.....$14.99
00100264 **114. Pride and Prejudice**......$9.99
00101612 **115. The Greatest Waltzes**.....$9.99
00287931 **116. A Star Is Born, La La Land, Greatest Showman & More**.$14.99
00289026 **117. Tony Bennett**................$14.99
00100136 **118. 100 Kids' Songs**...........$14.99
00139985 **119. Blues**.............................$12.99
00100433 **120. Bill & Gloria Gaither** ...$14.95
00100333 **121. Boogies, Blues & Rags**...$9.99
00100146 **122. Songs for Praise & Worship**........................$9.99
00100266 **123. Pop Piano Hits**............$14.99
00101440 **124. The Best of Alabama**......$7.95
00100001 **125. The Great Big Book of Children's Songs**..........$14.99
00101563 **127. John Denver**.................$12.99
00116947 **128. John Williams**...............$12.99
00140764 **129. Campfire Songs**..........$12.99
00116956 **130. Taylor Swift Hits**.........$10.99
00102318 **131. Doo-Wop Songbook**...$12.99
00100258 **132. Frank Sinatra: Christmas Collection** ..$10.99
00100306 **133. Carole King**..................$12.99
00100226 **134. AFI's Top 100 Movie Songs**.................$24.95
00289978 **135. Mary Poppins Returns** .$10.99
00291475 **136. Disney Fun Songs**........$14.99
00100144 **137. Children's Movie Hits**...$9.99
00100038 **138. Nostalgia Collection** ...$16.99
00100289 **139. Crooners** $19.99
00101956 **140. Best of George Strait** ...$16.99
00294969 **141. A Sentimental Christmas**.$12.99
00300288 **142. Aladdin**.......................$10.99
00101946 **143. Songs of Paul McCartney**.$8.99
00140768 **144. Halloween**...................$10.99
00100291 **145. Traditional Gospel**.......$9.99
00319452 **146. The Lion King (2019)**...$10.99
00147061 **147. Great Instrumentals** $9.99
00100222 **148. Italian Songs**...............$9.99
00329569 **149. Frozen 2**......................$10.99
00100152 **151. Beach Boys Greatest Hits**.$14.99

00101592 **152. Fiddler on the Roof** $9.99
00140981 **153. 50 Great Songs**............$14.99
00100228 **154. Walk the Line**..............$8.95
00101549 **155. Best of Billy Joel** $9.99
00101769 **158. Very Best of John Lennon**$12.99
00326434 **159. Cats** $10.99
00100315 **160. Grammy Awards Record of the Year 1958-2011**$19.99
00100293 **161. Henry Mancini**............$10.99
00100049 **162. Lounge Music** $10.95
00100295 **163. Very Best of the Rat Pack**$12.99
00277916 **164. Best Christmas Songbook**.$9.99
00101895 **165. Rodgers & Hammerstein Songbook**.................$10.99
00149300 **166. The Best of Beethoven**...$8.99
00149736 **167. The Best of Bach**...........$8.99
00100148 **169. Charlie Brown Christmas**$10.99
00100900 **170. Kenny Rogers**..............$12.99
00101537 **171. Best of Elton John**.........$9.99
00101796 **172. The Music Man** $9.99
00100321 **173. Adele: 21** $12.99
00100229 **175. Party Songs**..................$14.99
00100149 **176. Charlie Brown Collection** .$9.99
00100019 **177. I'll Be Seeing You** $15.99
00102325 **179. Love Songs of the Beatles**$14.99
00149881 **180. The Best of Mozart** $8.99
00101610 **181. Great American Country Songbook**....$16.99
00001246 **182. Amazing Grace**............$12.99
00450133 **183. West Side Story** $9.99
00290252 **184. Merle Haggard**...........$14.99
00100151 **185. Carpenters**..................$12.99
00101606 **186. 40 Pop & Rock Song Classics**...............$14.99
00100155 **187. Ultimate Christmas** $18.99
00102276 **189. Irish Favorites**...............$9.99
00100053 **191. Jazz Love Songs** $9.99
00123123 **193. Bruno Mars** $11.99
00124609 **195. Opera Favorites**............$8.99
00101609 **196. Best of George Gershwin** .$14.99
00119857 **199. Jumbo Songbook**..........$24.99
00295070 **200. Best Songs Ever** $19.99
00101540 **202. Best Country Songs Ever**.$17.99
00101541 **203. Best Broadway Songs Ever**...............$19.99
00101542 **204. Best Easy Listening Songs Ever** $17.99
00284127 **205. Best Love Songs Ever** ...$17.99
00101570 **209. Disney Christmas Favorites**...................$9.99
00100059 **210. '60s Pop Rock Hits** $14.99
14041777 **211. Big Book of Nursery Rhymes & Children's Songs**...$15.99
00126895 **212. Frozen** $9.99
00101546 **213. Disney Classics** $15.99
00101533 **215. Best Christmas Songs Ever**...............$22.99
00131100 **216. Frank Sinatra Centennial Songbook** .$19.99
00100040 **217. Movie Ballads**...............$9.99
00100156 **219. Christmas Songs with Three Chords** $9.99
00102190 **221. Carly Simon Greatest Hits**$8.95
00102080 **225. Lawrence Welk Songbook**$10.99
00283385 **234. Disney Love Songs**.......$12.99
00101581 **235. Elvis Presley Anthology** .$16.99
00100165 **236. God Bless America & Other Songs for a Better Nation**$26.99
00290209 **242. Les Misérables** $10.95
00100158 **243. Oldies! Oldies! Oldies!**$12.99
00100041 **245. Simon & Garfunkel** $10.99
00100267 **246. Andrew Lloyd Webber Favorites**.................$10.99
00100296 **248. Love Songs of Elton John**.$12.99
00102113 **251. Phantom of the Opera**..$14.99
00100203 **256. Very Best of Lionel Richie**$10.99
00100302 **258. Four-Chord Worship** $9.99
00286504 **260. Mister Rogers' Songbook**.$9.99
00100235 **263. Grand Irish Songbook** .$19.95
00100063 **266. Latin Hits** $7.95
00100062 **269. Love That Latin Beat**......$8.99
00101425 **272. ABBA Gold Greatest Hits**.$9.99
00100024 **274. 150 of the Most Beautiful Songs Ever**...$22.99

00102248 **275. Classical Hits** ....$8.9[9]
00100186 **277. Stevie Wonder** ....$10.9[9]
00100227 **278. 150 More of the Most Beautiful Songs Ever**...$24.99
00100236 **279. Alan Jackson** ....$20.9[9]
00100237 **280. Dolly Parton** ....$10.9[9]
00100238 **281. Neil Young** ....$12.9[9]
00100239 **282. Great American Songbook** ....$19.9[9]
00100068 **283. Best Jazz Standards Ever**.$15.9[9]
00281046 **284. Great American Songbook: The Singers**..................$19.9[9]
00100271 **286. CMT's 100 Greatest Love Songs**..................$24.9[9]
00100244 **287. Josh Groban** ....$14.9[9]
00102124 **293. Movie Classics** ....$10.9[9]
00100303 **295. Best of Michael Bublé** ...$14.9[9]
00100075 **296. Best of Cole Porter**........$9.9[9]
00102130 **298. Beautiful Love Songs** .....$9.9[9]
00100077 **299. The Vaudeville Songbook** .$7.9[9]
00259570 **301. Kids' Songfest**.............$12.9[9]
00110416 **302. More Kids' Songfest** ....$12.9[9]
00100275 **305. Rod Stewart** ....$12.9[9]
00102147 **306. Irving Berlin Collection** ..$16.9[9]
00100276 **307. Gospel Songs with 3 Chords**.....................$8.9[9]
00100194 **309. 3-Chord Rock 'n' Roll**....$9.9[9]
02501515 **312. Barbra Streisand**.........$10.9[9]
00100197 **315. VH1's 100 Greatest Songs of Rock & Roll**...........$19.9[9]
00100234 **316. E-Z Play® Today White Pages**..................$27.9[9]
00100277 **325. Taylor Swift** ....$10.9[9]
00100249 **328. French Songs**.................$8.9[9]
00100251 **329. Antonio Carlos Jobim** ...$7.9[9]
00102275 **330. The Nutcracker Suite**.....$8.9[9]
00100092 **333. Great Gospel Favorites**..$8.9[9]
00100273 **336. Beautiful Ballads**..........$19.9[9]
00100278 **338. The Best Hymns Ever** ...$19.9[9]
00100084 **339. Grease Is Still the Word**..$12.9[9]
00100235 **346. The Big Book of Christmas Songs**..........$16.9[9]
00100089 **349. The Giant Book of Christmas Songs**...........$9.9[9]
00100087 **354. The Mighty Big Book of Christmas Songs** .....$12.9[9]
00100088 **355. Smoky Mountain Gospel Favorites** ....$9.9[9]
00100093 **358. Gospel Songs of Hank Williams** ....$7.9[9]
00100095 **359. 100 Years of Song** ....$19.9[9]
00100096 **360. More 100 Years of Song**..$19.9[9]
00159568 **362. Songs of the 1920s** .....$19.9[9]
00159569 **363. Songs of the 1930s** .....$19.9[9]
00159570 **364. Songs of the 1940s** .....$19.9[9]
00159571 **365. Songs of the 1950s** .....$19.9[9]
00159572 **366. Songs of the 1960s** .....$19.9[9]
00159573 **367. Songs of the 1970s** .....$19.9[9]
00159574 **368. Songs of the 1980s** .....$19.9[9]
00159575 **369. Songs of the 1990s** .....$19.9[9]
00159576 **370. Songs of the 2000s** .....$19.9[9]
00339094 **370. Songs of the 2010s** $19.99
00100103 **375. Songs of Bacharach & David**...$9.9[9]
00100107 **392. Disney Favorites**.........$19.9[9]
00100108 **393. Italian Favorites** ....$9.9[9]
00100111 **394. Best Gospel Songs Ever**.$19.9[9]
00100115 **400. Classical Masterpieces** ..$11.99

HAL•LEONARD®

Prices, contents and availability subject to change without notice

042*
33